On Earth as in Heaven

Paul B. Stimson

High Tide Publications
Deltaville, Virginia

Copyright © 2014 by Paul B. Stimson

All rights reserved. No part of this publication may be reproduced, distributed or transmitted in any form or by any means, including photocopying, recording, or other electronic or mechanical methods, without the prior written permission of the publisher, except in the case of brief quotations embodied in critical reviews and certain other noncommercial uses permitted by copyright law. For permission requests, write to the publisher, addressed "Attention: Permissions Coordinator," at the address below.

High Tide Publications, Inc.
1000 Bland Point Road
Deltaville, Virginia 23043
www.HighTidePublications.com

Ordering Information:

Quantity sales. Special discounts are available on quantity purchases by corporations, associations, and others. For details, contact the "Special Sales Department" at the address above.

On Earth as in Heaven/Paul B. Stimson, 1st ed.

Printed in the United States of America

ISBN: 978-0-9884637-2-1

To Father Bill

Praetium caritatis tu[1]

Table of Contents

Foreword i
Introduction iii
Preface v
Acknowledgments ix

Chapter I - Spiritual Journeys: 1
   The Redeemer 2
   Stronger Than the Material Mended 4
   Brokenness 7
   Cleft Palate 10
   The Four-Flusher 16
   Kiwi Aeronautics 19
   Obedience 22
   Grace 25

   Reflection Questions Chapter I 28
      The Redeemer 28
      Stronger Than the Material Mended 28
      Brokenness 29
      Cleft Palate 29
      The Four-Flusher 30
      Kiwi Aeronautics 30
      Obedience 31
      Grace 31

Chapter II – Knowledge for the Heart 33
   Free Will 34
   Light & Darkness 37
   Suffering 39
   Amphetamines, Narcotics & Endorphins 42
   Trust & Trustworthiness 45
   The Judas Syndrome 47
   Anger Management 49
   Love is Never Having to . . . what? 52
   Hendrick's Journey 54
   A new twist on an old tale 54
   Forgiveness 58
   Fear & Fear 61
   Belonging & Longing 64
   Gratitude 66
   Meatballs 68

Table of Contents

Reflection Questions - Chapter II *71*
- Free Will 71
- Light & Darkness 71
- Suffering 72
- Amphetamines, Narcotics & Endorphins 72
- Trust & Trustworthiness 73
- The Judas Syndrome 73
- Anger Management 73
- Love Is Never Having to. . . What? 74
- Hendrick's Journey 74
- Forgiveness 75
- Fear & Fear 75
- Belonging & Longing 76
- Gratitude 76
- Meatballs 76

Chapter III – Knowledge for the Soul 78
- *Evil* *79*
- *The Power of Satan* *81*
- *The Will of God* *83*
- *Judgment Day* *86*
- *Was Jesus Christ sinless?* *91*
- *Incarnation* *94*
- *Faith* *97*
- *Predestination* *99*
- *Vulnerability* *101*
- *Worthiness* *104*
- *Blessed Be the Sin* *106*
- *What Would the Disciples Do?* *109*
- *Scarcity & Abundance* *112*
- *Sin & Sanctity* *115*
- *Mystery* *117*
- *Warts and All* *120*
- *Earth & Heaven* *123*
- *One Flesh* *125*
- *Come, Labor On.* *128*

Reflection Questions - Chapter III *130*
- Evil 130
- The Power of Satan 130
- The Will of God 131
- Judgment Day 131

Table of Contents

Was Jesus Christ Sinless?... 131
Incarnation.. 132
Faith... 132
Predestination 132
Vulnerability 133
Worthiness... 133
Blessed Be the Sin 133
What Would the Disciples Do? 134
Scarcity & Abundance 134
Sin & Sanctity.. 135
Mystery... 135
Warts and All 135
Earth & Heaven 136
One Flesh 136
Come, Labor On 137

Chapter IV – Knowledge for the Mind 139
Symbols of the Holy Trinity 140
Our Worm's-Eye View of Reality 144
Time & Eternity 147
The Spiritual Dimension 150
Either/Or versus Both/And 155
The Hebrew Scriptures 160
Temptation... 163
The Language of the Kingdom 166
Spoken Word, Written Word 169

Reflection Questions: Chapter IV 173
Symbols of the Holy Trinity 173
Our Worm's-Eye View of Reality............................... 173
Time & Eternity.. 174
The Spiritual Dimension.. 174
Either/Or Versus Both/And 174
The Hebrew Scriptures 175
Temptation.. 175
The Language of the Kingdom................................. 175
Spoken Word, Written Word 176

Chapter V – Churchy Stuff 177
Vocation... 178
Opposing God?.. 180
Advent.. 182

Table of Contents

Crisis in the Churches *185*
Evangelism.. *188*
Peter & Paul *191*
Beans & Rice *194*
Loaves & Fishes *197*
Tithing.. *200*
Big Ministries, Little Ministries *202*
Truth *205*
Interfaith Relations *208*
The E Word *213*
The Governance of the Church *215*
    Part I: the Unanimity Rule 215
    Part 2: The "High Five".. 218
Powers of Two *220*

Reflection Questions, Chapter V *223*
    Vocation 223
    Opposing God 223
    Advent... 224
    Crisis in the Churches 224
    Evangelism 224
    Peter & Paul.. 225
    Beans & Rice 225
    Loaves & Fishes.. 225
    Tithing 226
    Big Ministries, Little Ministries... 226
    Truth 226
    Interfaith Relations 227
    The E Word 227
    The Governance of the Church 227
    Part I: the Unanimity Rule 227
    Part II: the High Five 228
    Powers of Two 228

Chapter VI -Addenda.. **229**
Author's Notes **230**

Foreword

This book is not for you if you believe in a God, who makes lots of rules, and you feel you can live with these rules pretty well, and look forward to the day all those sinful people out there really get blasted.

If, on the other hand, you've been raised with a belief in that kind of God and it scares you, read on!

This book has been written by an ordinary Christian layman for ordinary laypersons. You may be active in the Church; you may be seeking, or you may be downright questioning. That's OK. You'll find this book readable and helpful in thinking through some basic issues of life, love, and eternity.

This book can be used for individual meditations or group discussion. Each article is brief, focuses on a single issue, and ends with several questions for reflection. Many articles contain vivid little images from everyday life that will grab attention and help make sense. Any of the reflection questions can lead you deeper, as far as you want to go.

The God[2] you will find in this book is a social God. After all, a god who is Father, Son, and Holy Spirit[3] (yet only one being) is bound to carry on an eternal conversation and wants to include you in that conversation. A personal relationship. Wow!

This God understands all the warts and distortions of human sin and is determined to help us grow into the persons he created us to be. He has a dream for each one of us and we each have a built-in emptiness as we live outside that dream. "There's gotta be more to life than this!"

This God created us in his own image and gave us freedom of choice (often called free will). He respects that freedom and seeks to win us by a love-based forgiveness that reaches the heart and calls us to be a new people. He invites us to develop into an eternity of loving relationships and provides the Way.

This book is an invitation to explore the Christian faith. The exploration is focused, as the subtitle suggests, on the issues of life, love, and eternity.

(The Rev'd.) R. Channing Johnson, PhD
Glendale, Arizona

Introduction

The evidence is clear: from prehistory right through the present; most cultures have had a deeply-held belief in a god or gods, ranging from powers and agricultural gods to a Supreme Being, and also in the afterlife. Some have called this the 'God gene;' surely our need to relate and our quest for belonging plays a role.

The variations in faith are wide. An early concept of an afterlife in Judaism was of a place, or a state of being, called Sheol, a faint semiconscious condition. The Pharaohs had themselves entombed in pyramids, provisioned with every imaginable necessity and luxury for the afterlife, including large boats. Some American Indians foresaw a "Happy Hunting Ground." Christianity holds out to us the promise of union with God and with the Saints who have gone before.

Most Supreme Beings have been seen as fierce, demanding and punishing. There is a widespread fear of not measuring up, of being left on the outside looking in. We squirm; we appease; we aim to please. Somehow we know it can never be enough.

The Father God revealed to us by Jesus Christ is not like this. No god conjured up in our imagination could ever be so totally different. God only takes us as we are, knowing that we are but dust, offering bounteous forgiveness and an unconditional, self-sacrificing love. We are asked to respond to that Love and reflect it into the world. From any other motive, good behavior counts for nothing.

I grew up in the Christian tradition, and many of these writings reflect that orientation. But advancing age has brought a broadening, and a recognition that Truth is Truth, from whatever perspective.

The pioneers of the Christian Way were accused of " . . . turning the world upside down." Modern writers increasingly point to the "upside-down" qualities of the Laws of the Kingdom of Heaven. Perhaps we have been standing on our heads all the while; surely the Kingdom of Heaven is right- side up and we, the latter-day followers of The Way, have a commission to upend the world.

Preface

My father once remarked that " . . . what people call paradox will probably turn out to be the Laws of the Kingdom of Heaven." These essays and parables point away from the age-old effort to make earthly "sense" of the Christian faith, and focus on the Bible's vision of the Kingdom in which loss is gain, meekness is power and servant hood is leadership. Gradually we come to see which end is up.

We have no time to waste, because the Kingdom of Heaven is not pie-in-the-Sky for some vague future: the Kingdom of Heaven is here and now—in the midst of us, within us. Of all the difficult sayings in Scripture—and, there are many—this is among the hardest, yet among the most important. The sayings are difficult to grasp only because we live our lives immersed in space and time, seeing only glimpses of the Kingdom of Heaven—which lies outside the bounds of space and time. That is the crux of it.

The writers of Scripture caught glimpses of Eternity. Psalm 90 says, "For a thousand years in thy sight are but as yesterday. . ." The second letter of Peter captures the paradox more fully: ". . . with the Lord, one day is as a thousand years, and a thousand years as one day."

Jesus, the Christ, came among us, knowing full well that his message sounds strange to Earth-bound ears. He used metaphor, simile and parable to convey those things which could not be expressed directly. "For now we see through a glass darkly,"[4] the King James Version puts it, "but then face- to-face. Now I know in part; then I shall understand fully, even as I have been fully understood."

Mathews, Virginia, USA
July 2007

This collection of articles has grown slowly over the past twenty-five years. There is, therefore, no thread of evolving argument; in most cases they stand alone. Friends who have read the manuscript and offered feedback have suggested that they work better on a one-a-day basis rather than read through.

The reflection questions have been added as an aid to group study. Please note that discussion of the questions is not a substitute for discussion of the article. It is recommended that the article be read aloud at the start of the session, followed by discussion—as-a-whole or paragraph-by-paragraph, as the Spirit leads. On this foundation, study of the questions, one-by-one, may then open new avenues.

Please note: the Reflection Questions, a vital element in this book, are still under construction. Suggested questions, thoughtful and thought-provoking, are welcome. Send a note to pstimson@juno.com

Acknowledgments

The author is grateful to countless friends over the years who have offered both critique and encouragement as this series of articles developed. More recently, several have watched over the development of the book, urging important revisions and, especially, adding to the Reflection Questions following each article. Notable among these are the Rev'd R. Channing Johnson, PhD, who has worked closely with me, clarifying my perspectives and overruling my heresies. Nina Eastman Buzby of Kingston Parish, Mathews, Virginia wrote most of the reflection questions. My son Mark Andrew Stimson painted the front cover and my son John Benjamin Stimson lettered it; also he drew three illustrations.

Chapter I-
Spiritual Journeys:
Some Virtual; Some Actual

Before the invention of written language, information exchange was by word-of-mouth. People must have discovered that a dry recitation of facts went in one ear and out the other, but story-telling could endure through the ages.

The Redeemer, the first article in this chapter, has been placed here for two reasons: it sets the tone for the book, and it is a living example of the power of story-telling. The story is actually not mine; in my youth I read it somewhere, possibly the Reader's Digest. I do not know whether it was presented as factual or fictional and I discover that it does not really matter. That was more than seventy years ago. After I started the series of articles that formed this book it popped up in memory, so vividly that I think the small details were mostly in the original.

Paul Stimson

The Redeemer

> *For our sake he made him to be sin who knew no sin, so that in him we might become the righteousness of God.*
> *(II Corinthians 5:21)*

A businessman stopped for the night at a small-town hotel. He had counted on getting one more squeeze out of his flattened toothpaste tube; alas, it simply wasn't there. Glancing out the window, he saw a dry-goods store across the street; with a grunt he pulled his pants back on and went out.

The layout of the store looked strange: a wall bisected the building, stretching from the back wall almost to the front door. There were two checkout counters straddling the wall, and the goods on each side looked much like the other. With a shrug, he went left and emerged a moment later with his toothpaste. Back in the lobby, the desk clerk provided the explanation—the sad story. Decades ago, two brothers had pooled their resources to establish the store. They had run it harmoniously for many years; at peak hours of the day they worked together while dividing up the slack

Chapter 1 – Spiritual Journeys: Some Virtual; Some Actual

hours. But one day the till came up short ten dollars, and each accused the other.

Tensions rose, and soon the stalemate was beyond reconciliation. The partition was built, and the separate cash registers set in place. Eager to avoid taking sides, the townspeople kept carefully tracked where they shopped. A few of them even kept a running total of their register receipts, in order to keep them in balance. Feeling fatigued from the unresolved tension and the strain of long working hours, the brothers seemed to be aging rapidly, but neither would soften.

Our traveler pondered a long moment, then re-crossed the street. Dusk was falling, and the brothers were preparing to close. Neither would ever leave before the other, and the two locks on the door took separate keys. With audible strain, in his voice he called the brothers to the front. Speaking barely above a whisper, he explained that years before he had stopped for the night and, finding himself out of toothpaste; he had come to the store. The till stood open, unattended, and he had succumbed to a dastardly impulse, plucking out a ten-dollar bill and slipping away unnoticed. His conscience had gnawed at him ever since, and he had on this trip come out of his way to make amends. Seizing the right hands of the brothers, he pressed them together with a ten-spot in between.

You may have guessed already that this was our Hero's first and only visit to this village.

Please discuss the content of the article before considering the Reflection questions, Page 28

Paul Stimson

Stronger Than the Material Mended

> *For it was fitting that [God], for whom and by whom all things exist, in bringing many sons to glory, should make the pioneer of their salvation perfect through suffering.*
> *(Hebrews 2:10)*

In my youth, I was fascinated with hardware stores. My weekly allowance in those Great-Depression years was one dime and one penny, so I wished a lot but bought little. *Stronger than the material mended*, proclaimed one brand of glue. I thought and thought about that claim: what a concept!

Decades later, I fractured a bone in my hand. As the doctor encased it in plaster, I wondered out loud how the bone could be aware that it was broken, how the new growth could 'know' where to reconstruct, cell upon cell. He had no answer, of course, but noted that if that bone ever takes another heavy hit, it probably will fail anywhere except at the site of this fracture. Stronger than the material mended!

The soft tissues of the hand were severely swollen by the injury, so it was not possible to set the bone straight. The doctor explained

Chapter 1 – Spiritual Journeys: Some Virtual; Some Actual

that bones are living tissue; over the years, new growth will concentrate on the inside of the bend, while old cells on the outside die off and are carried away. So, the bone will gradually straighten itself! Hard to believe, but that is just what has happened: the bend is much less pronounced than it was at first—and stronger to boot.

In the Spartan economy that Nature applies to all living things that which bears stress is reinforced and that which is idle atrophies. Some years ago I noticed that my ability to come up with the right word at the needed moment was slowing. I took up crossword puzzles, and firmly believe that it helped. 'Use it or lose it,' says the adage. We lap-of-luxury Americans still remember how to walk, but mostly because we have not yet devised an easier way to get to the garage. Athletes gain both muscle mass and muscle tone, and their bones grow stronger, too. Conversely, the first astronauts lost bone density at a prodigious rate in their weightless world. Strenuous exercise was mandated on later flights.

So let it be with the human psyche which, like the physical body, was designed to withstand a wide range of 'normal' stresses, but can be overwhelmed by crisis. Here, too, the basic tools and materials of healing are built-in. For body, mind and spirit alike, this internal first-aid kit is sometimes sufficient; in other cases the healing is faster if outside help is available.

Those of us old enough to remember the years of World War II can think back on the hardship of getting along on three gallons of gasoline per week and debating whether to use a red ration coupon on meat or butter. But too rarely did we think of those in war-torn

Europe, for whom a half-spoiled leaf of lettuce would have been luxury.

Suffering, much as we dread the thought, is the gymnasium, the treadmill, the exercise machine of the human soul. Even a modest regimen of self-discipline and self-deprivation can build the moral fiber essential to survival in hard times—which can take us by surprise, individually or en masse. Former senator Max Cleland, severely wounded in the Vietnam War, wrote a book titled Strong at the Broken Places[5], which jogged my memory of the glue bottle. In his book, *Man's Search for Meaning*[6], Viktor Frankl described first-hand the almost unimaginable suffering of the victims of the Holocaust, in which the hard-wired will-to-live was tested to its limits. Frankl emerged with the self-defining conclusion of his life: That which does not kill me makes me stronger.

Please discuss the content of the article before considering the Reflection questions, Page 28

Chapter 1 – Spiritual Journeys: Some Virtual; Some Actual

Brokenness

Make me to hear joy and gladness that the bones
which thou hast broken may rejoice.
(Psalm 51:8)

Broken is a strange, double-edged word. If we speak of a broken man, we mean one who has been dealt more woe than he can deal with, and whose life is seemingly over. But when we speak of a horse as broken, we mean that its wildness has come under control, and it is now fit for service. When the latter sense of brokenness is applied to the human condition, it becomes a key word in our spiritual journey.

When the foregoing essay, Stronger than the Material Mended, was in the first draft, I sent it to a friend for comment. The fullness and richness of his reply startled me; with permission, I quote an excerpt:

Excellent, Paul! Suffering is indeed the great treadmill of life. I don't share this with everyone, but I am a recovering alcoholic. I want to share something that I have heard many alcoholics with long-term sobriety say, and that is, "I am a grateful alcoholic." They were grateful that they had the disease of alcoholism, because without having had it they would have never been led to the joyful and satisfying life that they have today. The disease and the recovery made them strong and happy individuals, probably happier and more well-adjusted than they would have been if they had never had the disease.

Think of it—a person with a life-threatening illness, grateful for the disease? But what it all means is that the Twelve-Step program, which I believe to be God-inspired, has the power to convert brokenness in the first sense, above, into the second sense, which contains the key to a dedicated and meaningful life.

The response then referred to a paragraph in Alcoholics Anonymous, the master text which people in the Program call The Big Book. I borrowed a copy so I could quote it accurately[7]:

And acceptance is the answer to all my problems today. When I am disturbed, it is because I find some person, place, thing or situation—some fact of my life—unacceptable to me, and I can find no serenity until I accept that person, place, thing or situation as being exactly the way it is supposed to be at this moment. Nothing, absolutely nothing, happens in God's world by mistake. Until I could accept my alcoholism, I could not stay sober; unless I accept life completely on life's terms, I cannot be happy. I need to concentrate not so much on what needs to be changed in the world as on what needs to be changed in me and my attitudes.

Eloquently worded, it really boils down to a restatement of the Serenity Prayer, which is a cornerstone of the Program.

Now listen up, all who have an unearned, God-given sobriety, who thus have been spared the debilitating disease of addiction: just

Chapter 1 – Spiritual Journeys: Some Virtual; Some Actual

as it is not necessary to burn down a barn in order to roast the pig inside, I believe it possible to learn this type-two brokenness without enduring intoxication. One and all, we can find in the Twelve Steps a path to emotional and spiritual wholeness. Self-study works; probably study in some small-group setting will work better. You'll be glad you did.

Please discuss the content of the article before considering the Reflection questions, Page 29

Paul Stimson

Cleft Palate[8]

The Spirit of the Lord God is upon me because the Lord has anointed me to bring good tidings to the afflicted.
(Isaiah 61:1a KJV)

My father was born with a cleft palate. Nowadays that birth defect is surgically corrected in the first months of life and recovery is usually complete. But the year was 1899, and it was then customary to delay the surgery until about age five. During those critical years, the arch of the roof of his mouth was incomplete, and there was no separation between mouth and sinuses.

Human speech is formed by a complex interaction of mouth parts, resulting in air flow alternating between nose and mouth. When the palate is not able to modulate the flow, most of it exits the nose. Intelligibility suffers; especially, the sibilant sounds are weak or absent. Even after surgery, early speech patterns persisted, and the primitive speech therapy of that era helped little.

At home, they were used to it, but school days were hell. Kids pounce on each other's defects and weaknesses; it seems to be mostly for amusement, and most do not become aware of the cruelty

Chapter 1 – Spiritual Journeys: Some Virtual; Some Actual

until much later—if ever. They called him 'Yikyaw', because that was the closest he could come to saying his own name, 'Stimson.'

Home life was intellectually fertile, but it was a spiritual desert. In his teens, motivated by forces he didn't understand, he launched what can only be seen as a spiritual quest. In the churches, he saw a cacophony of competing claims; he widened his search to encompass as much of a worldwide religion as he could find. As he came to realize years later the quest was, at the conscious level, driven by intellect, and not much of value can be uncovered from that one-dimensional view. The underlying spiritual hunger was below his awareness.

In graduate school, he was told that he had the makings of a scholar, but would need to learn many more languages, ancient and modern, before he could get onto that track. He settled on a vision of becoming a world-renowned paragon of Comparative Religions; students then would come from far and wide to hear him lecture, sitting (figuratively) in a semicircle at his feet and straining to understand every misshapen syllable.

But aah—those languages, those formidable languages. Ancient languages, such as Aramaic, were not available at the university. His advisers sent him to a nearby Episcopal seminary, where he was made uncomfortable by his dark suspicion of clergy. Brusquely, he told them that he was there for languages and nothing, but languages, thank you. Graciously, they took him on his own terms. A new world unfolded before him; soon he started taking some of their regular courses, and within a year he was enrolled in the full curriculum. Still, there was no objective of the ministry in view: he was studying religion from his critical, historical point of view. He asked naive questions with eager curiosity, and studied with an intensity he had never thought possible. Digging words out of the lexicon, he read the gospels in Greek. Fitting words into sentences, he felt he was seeing Christ for the first time, as if he were present in Galilee, in Gethsemane and on Calvary. But the empty tomb, the appearances in the Upper Room and on the Emmaus Road stopped him cold. The difficult he handled easily; the impossible took a little longer.

Newly baptized; he soon saw that he was baptized into something—a functioning part of a greater whole. It is necessary to take sides. A man is not only known, but made, by the company he keeps. He felt that if he could at least marinate his soul in the Church, ancient, dignified, aesthetically beautiful, intellectually honest and fearless, no harm and possibly much good might come of it.

In his own words: "We come now to the climax. My mentor and friend, a young professor of Hebrew and Greek, was also curate of a church. When he asked me if I would be a lay reader, I was too shocked and frightened to speak. How could I, with such a defect that made class recitations an ordeal and meeting strangers a torture, be expected to read prayer and psalm and scripture in Church? Those things are beautiful; they are holy—I certainly could not read them. A dozen plausible excuses leaped into my mind. Of course, I said 'no.'

Chapter 1 – Spiritual Journeys: Some Virtual; Some Actual

"But then the strangest thing happened: I can only describe it pictorially; it was as if I were on a high diving board on a night so black that I could not even see the water beneath me, yet a Pressure from behind was gently willing me on to make the leap. I became his lay reader.

"Those first Sunday evenings were pretty awful. Then came a night when, as we were vesting, Bob asked if I had read tonight's lessons. 'Of course,' I replied. 'That 61st Isaiah,' he mused. 'If we could only make people hear that.'

"A shiver.

"The choir filed in. I can see the processional, the altar ablaze with candles, the Cross gleaming above us as we knelt. Anyone knowing the opening sentences of the Order for Evening Prayer will be with me in spirit. I probably never heard or said the Lord's Prayer, for that Pressure was there again. This time It showed me the waiting congregation and the lectern with the Book. This time It told me I was the link—the feeble link—between the two. And—I suppose I made the first real prayer of my life. It was not something 'thought' or 'said.' It was an act, an act of faith. If he willed these people to hear his Word through me they would hear, even through my voice.

"I stepped to the lectern with no time at all for reflection or understanding. I felt in mind and body and soul a sensation almost painfully exquisite. It was as if some heavy burden, carried for many weary miles, were suddenly gone.

"I read. Lost in the words of the great prophecy, I read:

Paul Stimson

The Spirit of the Lord God is upon me; because the Lord hath anointed me to preach good tidings unto the afflicted; he hath sent me to bind up the brokenhearted; to proclaim liberty to the captives, and the opening of the prison to those that are bound;

To proclaim the acceptable year of the Lord, and the day of vengeance of our God; to comfort all that mourn;

To appoint unto them that mourn in Zion, to give unto them beauty for ashes, the oil of joy for mourning, the garment of praise for the spirit of heaviness; that they might be called trees of righteousness, the planting of the Lord, that he might be glorified.

And they shall build the old washes; they shall raise up the former desolations, and they shall repair the waste cities, the desolations of many generations.

And strangers shall stand and feed your flocks, and the sons of the alien shall be your plowmen and your vine-dressers.

But you shall be named the Priests of the Lord: men shall call you the ministers of our God: ye shall eat the riches of the Gentiles, and in their glory shall ye boast yourselves.

"The service went on. I remember nothing of the rest of it, only a weariness and a peace. Finally came the recessional. As we two stepped into the sacristy, Bob turned. He looked on me with an expression I can never forget. He hugged me. 'Bob, what—?' I sputtered. 'Bill, don't you know? Your defect is gone. I have never heard Scripture read the way it was read tonight.'"

Only one outcome would be believable: he was ordained about the time I was cutting my first teeth, and the academic ambitions were abandoned. I never heard any hint of the former impediment; I noticed only that when he sang the movements of his mouth were strangely exaggerated—a vestige of his early struggle to be understood. Sadly, he saw himself ever after as a deeply flawed person. But look always for the paradox: I am convinced that his poor self-image ultimately opened him to be a clearer channel of God's Grace. It has been wisely said that God does not choose those who are fit; rather he fits those whom he has chosen. My father's deep sense of paradox, and of the power of parable, can be seen in the numerous citations of his thinking embedded in this book. He is the "Father Bill" who planted my seeds, and to whom I dedicate these essays and parables.

Decades later he reflected on his saga: "As I finish this paper I shall begin to prepare for tomorrow's early celebration of the Eucharist. Already I am eager to be saying what I have said thousands of times before*: I will go unto the altar of God, even unto the God of my joy and gladness: and upon the harp will I give thanks unto Thee, O God my God.* "My harp will be my voice."

Please discuss the content of the article before considering the Reflection questions, Page 29

Paul Stimson

The Four-Flusher[9]

> *Now, concerning spiritual gifts, brethren, I do not want you to be misinformed.*
> *(I Corinthians 12:1)*

Ten years prior, I had abruptly ceased going to Church. It was the decade of the Sixties which thinned the ranks of all the mainline churches. Of my own accord, I might never have taken that initiative, but watching the exodus raised the question of what was keeping me in. No answer echoed back, so I just drifted off. Now a new romance was incubating; my lady was deeply committed to the Faith. I had never resolved my own issues; I had concluded that Christianity was either far more important than I had found it to be, or not important at all. Now I wondered if Meg's faith might rub off on me.

A weekend retreat focused on the Gifts of the Spirit. The teaching was insightful and the discussion lively—maybe there is nourishment in this, after all? As the Sunday morning Eucharist approached, I was asked to select an epistle, and to read it. A silent gasp: truth be told; I didn't know an epistle from an apostle. I was dimly aware that the first four books of the New Testament were the gospels: was the rest of the volume all epistles? The search for a

Chapter 1 – Spiritual Journeys: Some Virtual; Some Actual

relevant reading would have taken days; I had mere minutes. If there had been an ounce of humility anywhere in me I would have declined the request, but just one word, "Sure," popped out of my mouth. Instantly, I felt an impulse to dart out and deflect those sound waves before they reached the nearest ear.

With no other recourse, I played dartboard. I opened the Bible to a point near the back, to be sure I didn't land in the Old Testament. My finger found a verse in the book of Revelation, which had no possible bearing on anything. Feverishly, I flipped a half inch of pages and stabbed again, reading, "Now there are varieties of gifts, but the same Spirit, and there are varieties of service, but the same Lord . . . " (I Corinthians 12:4) Years later, I was still unable to find a more appropriate reading for that occasion.

It has been wisely said that Justice is getting what you deserve; Mercy is not getting what you deserve, and Grace is getting what you do not deserve. As I stepped to the lectern, my body, mind and spirit were awash in such Grace as I had never before known. Seemingly, the words on the page entered a pipeline which passed through my eyes, brain, vocal cords and mouth, without my active participation. They emerged with a fervor, an earnestness, a resonance that had not previously been mine. After the service people commented on my reading, and that had never before happened.

Over the following days, a new message sifted into my consciousness: "Okay, Four-flusher[10]; that was a freebie. Now go out and learn how."

Paul Stimson

Please discuss the content of the article before considering the Reflection questions, Page 30

Chapter 1 – Spiritual Journeys: Some Virtual; Some Actual

Kiwi Aeronautics

The wings of the ostrich wave proudly; but are they the pinions and plumage of love?
(Job 39:13)

My late brother John Michael (1933–1999) once showed me a poem by Thomas Hardy, titled "The Impercipient"[11]—proper British for "one who does not perceive." In it, Hardy agonizes over the quandary of desiring to understand but simply being unable:

Why thus my soul should be consigned to infelicity,

Why always must I feel as blind to sights my brethren see, Why joys they've found I cannot find, abides a mystery.

John was hesitant to show it to me because I had a long history of responding hurtfully in any discussion of his agnosticism. I surprised him (and myself!) by telling him that I understood very well: I have been there.

Our father was a priest: a man of abiding faith, but with a persistent need to shore up the intellectual side of it. He cultivated friendships with priests of towering intellect—men who (as I see it) knew about God at the expense of a relationship with God. John locked into that mode of belief at an early age and rapidly got good at it. For a long time, he was intent upon seminary and ordination. Life then took a sharp turn for the worse, and in the collapse of his education, his career, his relationships and his mental health, he got furious at God—if, indeed, there was a God—for so mistreating him (or, perhaps, even for allowing him to be so mistreated.) The Hardy poem was the first sign I had seen in thirty years that he even desired to believe.

At the climax of the poem, Hardy asks if a bird deprived of wings stays on the ground by choice. The short answer, of course, is "yes." The penguin and the kiwi, the ostrich and the emu, show clear signs of ancestors who could fly, but chose not to, thus losing the ability. But in relation to the issue of faith, this short answer is the wrong answer, only because the wrong question has been asked.

I was for many years a member of the "believing" crowd so envied by Hardy. My own crisis of faith was still in the future; I simply didn't know that I didn't know. Thinking back to the pew-sitters around me, I am quite sure I wasn't the only one. Hardy seems not to have realized it, but in coming to know that he didn't know, he was a long step ahead of those he envied. "God has no grandchildren," the saying goes: I doubt it is likely to emerge from the Faith of our Fathers to an encounter with the Living God without a time of crisis.

I suggest that we are not birds, but kites: aerodynamically shaped but wingless. Birds fly actively; kites fly passively. The kite's only active moves are turning to face the Wind and the consent to lift off. Laden as we are with ballast and baggage, it may

Chapter 1 – Spiritual Journeys: Some Virtual; Some Actual

take a stiff breeze to get us airborne. As we learn to cast off those things we cannot keep in favor of things we cannot lose, we will fly high in a Zephyr.

The kite string is a vital part of the image. We hear of people " . . . so heavenly minded that they are no earthly good." The kite flies with its head in the clouds, and its feet planted firmly on Earth.

Please discuss the content of the article before considering the Reflection questions, Page 30

Obedience

> *I am the Lord your God . . .*
> *You shall have no other gods before me.*
> *(Exodus 20:2-3)*

Father David's face radiated the light of Christ as we sat talking far into the evening. His black cassock—the "uniform" of his monastic order—was rumpled and threadbare; he appeared to be a man who had risen above all worldly desires.

Somehow the conversation had turned to the three monastic vows, of poverty, chastity and obedience. I could scarcely believe what I heard when he told me that he had found poverty and chastity relatively easy. Then his eyes rolled back into his head: "...but uhhh, obedience!" I had always imagined that poverty and chastity must be the tough ones, and obedience not so difficult thereafter.

Who is perfectly, unquestioningly obedient? The only living creature that comes to mind is a well-trained dog—and many dog-owners pride themselves on that canine quality above all others. The ultimate example is a Seeing-Eye[12] dog, who understands the master's dependency and single-mindedly does its duty.

Chapter 1 – Spiritual Journeys: Some Virtual; Some Actual

I once interviewed Tony, a man blind since childhood, who was justly proud of his dog's training and the relationship that had developed between them. He told me of one key episode in which they had started home from his office in the late afternoon. Tony didn't know that there had just been a cloudburst, and the street was flooded. The dog paused at the curb; Tony insisted and was quickly ankle-deep. Thus he learned that there are times when he must obey his perfectly obedient dog. What a vision of leadership we can draw from this story!

All human society is organized on the premise that there must be rules governing behavior and that certain individuals must be in a position of formulating and enforcing those rules. There must also be an underlying system—a philosophy of government. Numerous systems have been tried throughout the history of the world, and all have worked imperfectly, simply because people are imperfect.

Our present system demands that a leader be visionary, and (somewhat paradoxically) be responsive to the will of the people. It seems that most people, most of the time, think that their view is better than anyone else's, even when that perspective is deeply flawed. (My mother once gave me a little placard that read: Be reasonable: Do it my way.) And inescapably, self-interest gets in the way of every earthly leader's judgment—the more so if the leader is not aware of the conflict.

Voting as we do out of narrow self-interest, it is no wonder that we elect so many leaders who see all decisions as a personal popularity contest. The perfectly obedient Jesus gave us a better template when he said: . . . *whoever would be first among you must be your slave (Matthew 20:27).*

Suppose there arose among us a leader with infinite vision of our best interests, who unfailingly understood our wants, needs and hopes, and whose self-interest absolutely never got in the way. Suppose we came to see that every time we thought we had a better way, we wound up worse off. Do you think we could learn to set aside our own worm's-eye view? Maybe we could, but evidently we won't, because such a leader is here and now. His Name is God.

Please discuss the content of the article before considering the Reflection questions, Page 31

Grace

> *What then? Are we to sin because we are not under law but under grace? By no means! ...But thanks be to God, that you who were once slaves of sin have become obedient from the heart to the standard of teaching to which you were committed, and, having been set free from sin, have become slaves of righteousness.*
> *(Romans 6:15-17)*

Civil society, at its best, keeps order by dispensing justice. At its worst, it is hardly civil. Fear of consequences keeps most people in line most of the time. Mercy, unevenly applied, lightens the load for some. Grace is largely a foreign concept.

It has been said that justice is getting what you deserve; mercy is not getting what you deserve, and grace is getting what you do not deserve. Justice may change behavior but grace changes hearts, with potentially far greater impact on behavior. Decades ago, I was an associate of an Episcopal order of nuns. I wanted to go on a weekend retreat but could not afford it; I was offered a free place in exchange for kitchen duties.

Paul Stimson

Sunday breakfast was to be pancakes and bacon. Saturday evening the nun in charge of the retreat house searched all the refrigerators and found only a little bacon — it was not nearly enough for the crowd. She decided it would have to do.

Sunday morning I was up early, mixing batter and frying bacon while the others were in Chapel. I have always been an incurable nibbler while cooking; I joke to myself that I am sampling for quality-control purposes. Also, I am addicted to bacon. I restricted myself to tiny fragments as they came out of the pan, but I ate too many of them, so the toll was significant. At serving time, I stacked the paltry pile of bacon on a saucer for people to help themselves as I dispensed the pancakes. I shouldn't have been surprised by the result, but I was: after the last person was served there was still much bacon on the saucer. I took it into the dining room and offered it around, but the consensus was that it should be an extra treat for the cook! Suddenly I felt very small, but gratefully accepted it.

This episode was a turning point in my spiritual life. I began to understand Grace as I never before had. And, just as I was preparing to write about it, I read of a young boy who had a passion for comic books. He spent hours in the corner drug store reading some, buying a few, but tucking some inside his shirt. One day his father saw the stack, estimated that there were more than his allowance could have afforded, so confronted him. The druggist listened to the youngster's trembling confession, disappeared for a moment and returned with a large ice cream sundae for him. End of thefts: sometimes Grace has its pragmatic side.

Chapter 1 – Spiritual Journeys: Some Virtual; Some Actual

I recall hearing of two late Nineteenth-Century altar boys, at different times and in different churches, who committed the colossal crime of spilling the chalice. In one case the priest said not a word but set about cleaning up; in the other the hapless youth was banished. The first grew up to be the renowned Bishop Fulton Sheen; the second was Joseph Broz, who later renamed himself Marshall Tito, ruling tyrannically over Yugoslavia for decades.

Is there a pattern somewhere here?

Please discuss the content of the article before considering the Reflection questions, Page 31

Reflection Questions Chapter I

The Redeemer

1) When has learning the rest of the facts changed your opinion?
2) How do misunderstandings escalate into feuds? How can they be prevented or resolved?
3) Is this peace-maker (Matthew 2:9) to be blessed for his act of reconciliation even though it includes a lie?
4) William Blake[13] wrote, "A truth that's told with ill intent/ Beats all the lies you can invent." Contrast a white lie for good and honorable purpose against a truth told for destructive purpose.
5) Consider: there is often a price to be paid for reconciliation: sometimes ten dollars; sometimes a Cross.

Stronger Than the Material Mended

1) Is it better to avoid difficulties or go through them?
2) What spiritual tools does God promise to give us in times of trouble?
3) Think of an example of a tough time which made you stronger.

Chapter 1 – Spiritual Journeys: Some Virtual; Some Actual

4) Think of an example of a tough time which might have made you stronger if you had known then what you know now.

Brokenness

1) What experience have you had of a wildness in yourself that needed to be broken before you could become a whole/healthy human being?
2) When has a time of brokenness in your life become a stepping stone to deeper spirituality?
3) II Corinthians 12:7-10 compares pride with grace. How can your weaknesses actually be strengths?
4) Think of a time when your strength got in the way of the Will of God.

Cleft Palate

1) Fully 20% of the verses in the four Gospels are devoted to miraculous healing. Can you accept this as part of your reality, even when we cannot understand how?
2) What do you perceive are your weaknesses?
3) Can you offer up your weaknesses, so that God may transform them into strengths?
4) Do you believe in miracles?

The Four-Flusher

1) When has God's Grace taken you by surprise?
2) God also has justice and mercy in his toolbox. Can you see that grace is always his first choice?
3) Perhaps we ought not to ask what experience people have but to seek out how they have been gifted and help them find their ministry.

Kiwi Aeronautics

1) What ballast in your life keeps you steady? What weighs you down?
2) Think of times when you have been able to soar: what contributed to your lift off?
3) Do you hunger for more awareness of the Presence of God?
4) Do you have the wings of an ostrich—good for show but not for flight? Do you want to fly?
5) How might an encounter with the Living God affect the way you live?
6) Are you practical, skeptical, down-to-earth? What might you be missing?
7) A prayer to the Holy Spirit: "Come, Holy Wind; lift my kite."

Chapter 1 – Spiritual Journeys: Some Virtual; Some Actual

Obedience

1) If you made a pie chart of your time spent, what would be the labels on the slices and how big would each slice be?
2) If your life were perfectly obedient to God's call, considering your unique gifts and longings, how different would the chart look?
3) The rabbis list over 600 unique commandments in the Torah, and some of them seem to conflict. Which ones do you choose to follow?
4) The temptation of Eve in the Garden of Eden began with a question: is there anything God has told you not to do?
5) At the Last Supper, Jesus gave a single Commandment for people of the New Covenant, to " . . . love one another as I have loved you." What would obedience to this commandment mean?

Grace

1) In what situations might justice be enough of a motivator?
2) Does mercy motivate you to stay in line? Why or why not?
3) .What would determine if the druggist's reaction was mercy or grace?
4) Can you give an example of a time when you were saved by grace?
5) Can you give an example of a time when receiving grace would have changed your path?

6) What things need to be present for grace to change a person's heart?

Chapter II – Knowledge for the Heart

The Ancients were intensely curious about the interior of the body, where and how its functions took place. The heart, for example, was taken to be the seat of some strong emotions because it goes all a-flutter when romance is in the air, and it pounds heavily when we are afraid. Only later did we learn that it is merely a blood pump. Despite this knowledge, the earlier conclusions and meanings are here to stay.

In the core of this book, we address the trinity of heart, soul and mind. The components are not actually separable, as is also the case in the three Persons of the Holy Trinity, but our gaze settles on one and then another.

The heart is the focus of earliest experience. When the eyes of parent and infant meet, hearts are joined

Paul Stimson

Free Will

> *If you continue in my word, you are truly my disciples, and you will know the truth, and the truth will make you free.*
> *(John 8:31-32)*

*T*he Golden Rule is a disarmingly simple pointer to best behavior: Do unto others as you would have them do unto you. Have you ever pondered what a world we would have if absolutely everyone absolutely always stopped to ponder every action, great and small, for its harmony with the Golden Rule? Think of it: there would be no violence, anyone who is cold or hungry would be helped, and the lock-and-key wouldn't have been invented.

Now, don't you imagine that God, all-knowing and all-powerful, considered the possibility of forming us so as to have no choice in the matter? I am quite sure that he not only has thought of it; he has done something quite like that in every anthill and every hive of honey bees. They display a strong sense of community; they specialize in various tasks for the well-being of that community. They maintain and defend their shelter and gather food for the winter. We cannot imagine a worker bee getting angry with the

Chapter II – Knowledge for the Heart

queen and sneaking down in the night to sabotage the new honeycomb. The plain truth is that insects are programmed to do a few simple things wondrously well; they clearly are not creatures of free will.

It is equally clear that God created many species larger and more complex than insects, with far more mental horsepower, but in some essential ways closer to the insects than to humans. God could have created us by that same pattern. But the opening of Genesis tells us that we are set apart; God made us in his own image. (1:26)

A fine point which must not be overlooked is that the properties we take to be uniquely human are transferable to other species. Our dogs, cats and horses clearly respond to our love, and in some ways they outshine us. C. S. Lewis remarked that to them; we must appear as gods[14]. We are not uniformly worthy of that awe.

The bottom line is that God made us free because, without freedom, there is no love. The choice to love is in the context of choice not to love. God is, of course, free; we know in our gut that he could at any time, with or without cause, decide not to love us. I think that we live in such dread of that possibility that, without really thinking about it, we probe the limits. In spite of the dreadful consequences, it would somehow be a relief to discover that he will take just so much, and that, once having been banished, we could pass the word back to the rest of the world that you can get away with this, and this, but don't do that, or you are over the edge.

The path to spiritual maturity includes learning that there is no edge. God, is free to draw the line anywhere, in addition, God may choose to draw it nowhere. Once we have grasped this, we have glimpsed the boundlessness of Love, and maybe, just maybe, we can start responding in freedom, not fear. Love and fear are mutually exclusive; the one tends to drive out the other. (Don't misunderstand; I am distinguishing fear from awe.)

Which brings us to the paradox-of-the-month: In the Kingdom of Heaven, freedom is used solely as the path to surrender. All-powerful God uses freedom as a means of surrendering to us, in death on the Cross. We must at some point come to see: ...For the foolishness of God is wiser than men, and the weakness of God is stronger than men . . . God chose what is foolish in the world to shame the wise; God chose what is weak in the world to shame the strong. (I Corinthians 1:25, 27). Foolish: that is the key word. At the Pearly Gates, Jesus throws his arms around us, sharing with us tears of sorrow and tears of laughter. In the Kingdom of Heaven, Joy and Sorrow fuse paradoxically, poignantly, into one.

Please discuss the content of the article before considering the Reflection questions, Page 71.

Chapter II – Knowledge for the Heart

Light & Darkness

In him, there is no darkness at all. The night and the day are both alike. The Lamb is the Light of the City of God Shine in my heart, Lord Jesus.
(Kathleen Thomerson)[15]

In the waning days of winter, we lean toward the light. Most of us find the short days and persistent overcast of winter to be depressing to some degree; in some it is so severe as to have earned a medical label: "SAD"--for Seasonal Affective Disorder. In Easter, the imagery of God, (the Creator of Light), and of Christ, (the Light of the World), blazes before us, coinciding with spring when new life breaks ground all around us.

In our simple-minded ways, we mostly associate darkness with fear, the unknown and evil. We spend vast sums on street lighting in hope of dispelling the lurking evil. We note that Judas Iscariot did his dastardly deed under cover of darkness. It is all too easy to dismiss the darkness, assigning it to be Satan's domain, and to avoid it. But let us look deeper: In the opening verses of Genesis, God names the darkness as well as the light, thus taking dominion over both.

Paul Stimson

A poem (author unknown) says it all:
One talked with me and I with him: "
We know Thou art the Light,"
I said, "But this is night And our whole world's abrim
With hideous shadows that shut out the land.
We know Thou art the Light,
But this is night . . .
When wilt Thou understand?" 'Twas then he bade me hark:
"Since I have come back from the dead, '
Though still the Light I'm something more he said:
I am the Dark."

Philosophers tell us that nothing exists without its opposite. Thus, if the whole universe were uniformly flooded with light, filling every crack, every closet, we could have no concept of light, let alone the darkness. Is a fish aware of the water in which it swims? Darkness is a place of rest. It is also a place of intimacy, both physical and spiritual. In my 'teens I read a verse (author unknown) which has never left me:

Darkness comes.
The dear darkness comes creeping
As I lie down with God.
And the wonderful feel of the darkness
Is like touching God.

Please discuss the content of the article before considering the Reflection questions, Page 71

Chapter II – Knowledge for the Heart

Suffering

> *For it was fitting that he, for whom and by whom*
> *all things exist, in bringing many sons to glory,*
> *should make the pioneer of their salvation*
> *perfect through suffering.*
> *(Hebrews 2:10)*

Walking in the woods on a cool, spring day, you see a large chrysalis attached to a twig. Intrigued, you break it off and put it in your pocket. Later you set it in front of the family photo on your desk and watch it, day by day, for signs of life. Finally one morning you hear a faint sound, and look up to see a crack form down one side of the chrysalis. The crack widens, and soon the underbelly of the butterfly is visible. Progress then seems to halt, 'though the critter struggles mightily.

Can you resist picking up the desk scissors and extending the crack, maybe just a little? I hope you will resist, because in the wondrous complexity of nature's ways, the butterfly needs the struggle of breaking out, to tone its muscles and jump-start its vascular system. If you interfere, it may tumble out and die.

We live in an age and culture which sees pain and suffering as mainly a negative thing—something which interferes with life, and which must be neutralized so we can get on with living. If we think any deeper, we mostly wonder why a loving God would allow suffering in the world. We may even conclude that God either is not all-powerful or not all-loving. Most of us cannot see any failure of love, so settle for seeing him less than all-powerful. This reasoning ducks some major issues. Foremost, God desires that we love. Since love is a choice, not just a warm, gushy feeling, we are faced equally with a choice not to love. Without that freedom, love could not exist. A computer could be programmed to utter the language of love, but no loving person would be fooled. It takes no great stretch to see how much of the world's suffering is rooted in the down-side of that choice, the decision not to love.

But much of the world's suffering has long been blamed directly on God. When Jesus was asked, "Who sinned, this man or his parents, that he was born blind?" (John 9:2), the question reflected the age-old view (still very much with us!) that God metes out punishment as a deterrent to sin—and that the punishment includes a withholding (even a denial) of his love. All too often, frail human love does seem to have this conditional quality—and the withholding of love is far more painful, far more damaging than any punishment. Who among us can unquestioningly believe with the Psalmist?

If they violate my statutes and do not keep my commandments,

Then I will punish their transgression with the rod and their iniquity with scourges;

Chapter II – Knowledge for the Heart

But I will not remove [them] from my steadfast love, or be false to my faithfulness.

(Psalm 89, vv. 31–34)

God can and will use everything that is and everything that happens, toward the working out of his purpose in the world. (See Romans 8:28). If we live long enough, we may even come to see that, in the upside-down Laws of the Kingdom, there is no "bad thing" beyond God's redeeming power.

Please discuss the content of the article before considering the Reflection questions, Page 72.

Paul Stimson

Amphetamines, Narcotics & Endorphins

> *"All things are lawful for me," but not all things are helpful. "All things are lawful for me," but I will not be enslaved by anything . . . Do you not know that your body is the temple of the Holy Spirit within you? So glorify God in your body.*
> *(I Corinthians 6:12,19,20)*

Excitement, numbness and contentment: we have known since before history that these are feelings that stem from within us. Also, we see scattered throughout God's green earth numerous forms of flora which can alter our moods when ingested. It is only in the past few decades that we have begun to learn how it all works: that our nervous systems are equipped with a wide range of receptors into which these complex chemicals can fit as keys fit locks. It is also clear that the receptors are there because the body secretes many mood-altering substances; the plant extracts in question merely mimic our natural secretions. The significant difference is that the external types can be taken on demand, instead of awaiting the complex mind-body-spirit interactions which generate them naturally.

Chapter II – Knowledge for the Heart

Amphetamine and narcotic are almost dirty words by now. While they have legitimate uses in pharmacology, they (along with many other "street drugs") are notable mainly for their place in illegal self-medication. Amphetamines can spice up a dull life, and a narcotic anesthetizes the rough edges of living.

Seemingly, the most deeply needed yet least sought after of the psychoactive substances are the endorphins. The big problem is that we cannot ingest them; we have to work for them. Surely they are the source of the well-known second wind of the distance runner— the stage in which the early fatigue suddenly lifts and every stride just feels good. I think also of the overwhelming feeling of euphoria in the wake of a good belly laugh. Long before Norman Cousins' adventure in stemming the tide of a life- threatening illness with old slapstick movies, the Reader's Digest was running a monthly page titled Laughter: the Best Medicine. Endorphins flood the system as we cuddle an infant, dance with a beloved partner, sing, and worship our Lord.

In the severe economy of all natural systems, what is not needed does not get built. My hunch is that an infant deprived of cuddling and coddling has few endorphins in the bloodstream; therefore, fewer-than-normal endorphin receptors develop. It might be that such a person is predisposed to depression or withdrawal from interaction with people.

We have been told that our feelings are not subject to conscious control: we cannot brush away sadness by deciding to be happy. In the short term that is doubtless true, but there is a lot of evidence pointing to real, long-term changes linked to our attitudes. The idea becomes believable in light of our growing knowledge that feelings are not so much abstractions as they are biochemistry.

In an ideal world, all children would grow up knowing they are loved and wanted, by their parents, their neighbors and God. I presume that our body chemistry would be in far better balance, and there would be little craving for mood-altering chemicals. Short-term solutions seem not to have much effect, whether by law enforcement forewarning of the dangers. The many facets of a long-term solution boil down to a single, life-long mission: learning to love.

Please discuss the content of the article before considering the Reflection questions, Page 72.

Chapter II – Knowledge for the Heart

Trust & Trustworthiness

Simon, son of John, do you love me?..
Feed my sheep.
(John 21:17)

Jesus chose Peter to lead the disciples (Matthew 16:18). From our worm's-eye view, we might presume that Peter had, over a long period, demonstrated his trustworthiness so as to earn that trust. Following that logic, we should fully expect that Peter, after fulfilling his Lord's prophesy of thrice denying him (Matthew 26:34; 69–75), would be bumped down to eleventh place, just above the self-destructive Judas Iscariot (Matthew 27:5).

The Father of the Prodigal (Luke 15:11 –32) surely knew that his two sons were quite different from each other. He also knew that neither of them had much spiritual maturity. Given the degree of personal sacrifice involved and the obvious danger to his son's health and safety, how many parents among us would have such foolish wisdom as to grant the younger son's request?

Consider, too, Charlie Brown's[16] perennial encounters with the mischievous Lucy van Pelt. Every time Charlie disbelieves her promise to hold the football, Lucy finds a new way of persuading him that this time will be different. We laugh at Lucy's diabolical cleverness and Charlie's foolish trust.

What do these three snapshots have in common?

- From anyone else, Peter could rightly expect a scolding for his gutlessness and a lecture about qualifications for leadership.
- From anyone else, the Prodigal could expect cautionary words about the world, warnings about self-indulgence and an exhortation to get on with helping his "mature and trustworthy" brother run the farm.
- From anyone else, the hellion Lucy should expect a firm "never again"

But in the Laws of the Kingdom of Heaven, trust is not "earned" through trustworthiness: in the upside-down Kingdom, trustworthiness is called forth by a deluge of unmerited trust. "Feed my Sheep," said Jesus to the broken Peter, the crestfallen Peter.

The father of the Prodigal paid a high price, but knew that his son would return, transformed—if he survived. (And how is it that he saw him "a great way off?" We can be quite sure that he watched all day, every day.)

The sanctified Charlie Brown knows that the cost of trust betrayed is high, but the price of trust denied is higher still.

Have you noticed that these three illustrations of a Law of the Kingdom of Heaven "happened" here on earth? Time's a-wastin'.

Please discuss the content of the article before considering the Reflection questions, Page 73.

Chapter II – Knowledge for the Heart

The Judas Syndrome

> *And throwing down the pieces of silver in the temple, [Judas] departed, and he went and hanged himself.*
> *(Matthew 27:5)*

The Apostles often failed to grasp what Jesus was trying to get across to them, but how often did misunderstanding progress to actual missteps or misdeeds? Two individuals readily come to mind: we treasure Simon Peter for his boyish over-enthusiasm, ever causing his reach to exceed his grasp, even earning a sharp rebuke from the boss (Matthew 16:23). But all through his discipleship the purity of his motive shines through: all love, always. Not so with Judas Iscariot, suspected of dipping into the till (John 12:6) and eventually committing history's most atrocious betrayal. From their opposite behavior in the wake of these wrongs we can draw a vivid understanding of the difference between repentance and remorse. Peter was restored, even enhanced; Judas took his own life.

The emotionally and spiritually mature among us, most of times, whether or not religiously motivated, are able and willing to face up to our wrongs and ask forgiveness. It is a hallmark of maturity. It works up to a point, but I am guessing that many of us can look back at one or more episodes that went so horribly wrong that the lights went out. "I am not the kind of person who could have done that," says Pride. "Oh yes you are, and then some," says the inner Judas.

Some seek to bury the whole thing, severing ties with the offended, even making irreversible decisions that make the burial deeper. Perhaps it is a tragic loss. If the quest for reconciliation is to be considered, the specter of rejection must be faced.

But that rejection, should it come, must be seen as the other person's problem. The antidote to the Judas Syndrome is courageous love. Loving courage must ever be the better course. Step Nine of the Twelve Steps of Alcoholics Anonymous urges that we make ". . .direct amends to such people wherever possible," but adds an important caveat, ". . .except when to do so might injure them or others."

Many waters cannot quench love; neither can floods drown it.

(Song of Solomon 8:7)

Please discuss the content of the article before considering the Reflection questions, Page 73.

Chapter II – Knowledge for the Heart

Anger Management

> *He who is slow to anger has great understanding,*
> *but he who has a hasty temper exalts folly.*
> *(Proverbs 14:20)*

Is anger a sin? It seems that there are many people who believe it is. Some mistranslations of the Seven Deadly Sins[17] list anger as one of the seven, but the Latin word is better translated as wrath, ire or malice, implying anger festering underground and resurfacing in inappropriate ways. But anger is actually one of the four basic emotions; anger and the other three (sorrow, fear and joy) are precious gifts from God and foundation stones of personality. They are easily remembered as mad, sad, scared and glad. All these are available for our use and subject to our misuse. It is natural for a child to lash out in anger at anyone or anything that is seen as a threat to comfort or security. Since the child is not able to do harm, a parent or guardian needn't feel threatened, thus can readily respond in a helpful way. But if the child fails to outgrow that primitive response, the dynamics change. An outburst of anger induces anger or fear or both in others and the episode can be painful and damaging. What is at issue here is not anger per se, but the mismanagement of anger. Anger is complex: it often contains elements of fear or sorrow, or both. In trying to understand anger, we do well to ask, "What am I afraid of, and what am I sad about?" The answers don't necessarily have a calming effect, but they are elements of a toolkit for anger management.

"When angry, count ten before you speak; if very angry, count a hundred." With this proverb, Thomas Jefferson drew the vital distinction between hot anger and tempered anger, and gave us the formula for converting the one into the other. Hot anger is beyond the reach of anger management.

Let us ponder for a moment Mohandas K. Gandhi and Martin Luther King, Jr., two of the most noteworthy leaders of movements for social change in the 20th Century. Both were born into despised, oppressed minority cultures, where any outcry or opposition was severely suppressed. There, repressed anger festered, occasionally boiling over in riots that left everyone worse off. Gandhi and King had the vision and the wisdom to see that fighting fire with fire would never work, so they sought an alternative. Both were familiar with the Christian Scriptures, and there they found their cue:

Repay no one evil for evil, but take thought for what is noble in the sight of all. If possible, so far as it depends on you, live peaceably with all. Beloved, never avenge yourselves but leave it to the wrath of God, for it is written, "Vengeance is mine, I will repay says the Lord." No, "if your enemy is hungry feed him; if thirsty give him drink; for by so doing you will heap burning coals upon his head," Do not be overcome by evil, but overcome evil with good. (Romans 12:17-21)

Chapter II – Knowledge for the Heart

So, non-violent resistance and civil disobedience became major forces for change. For Gandhi and King, to infuse this principle into their own personalities was one thing, but to inspire and impel the masses was quite another. Force of personality was the key for both; deep-seated anger, redirected to its God-given purpose, spread to many of those who heard them. The forces of evil were bewildered by marchers who refused to fight back. "Noble in the sight of all" is a key phrase: it seems that people who do not monitor their own behavior, thus are mindlessly evil, are taken aback by mindful good. The results of these movements were uneven and will never reach perfection, but they are here to stay.

A minor episode in my youth transformed my attitude toward highway manners. The day was sweltering, and the road congested; when a car tried to merge in front of me I leaned on my horn. Abruptly the driver slowed and let me pass; as I scowled he waved me on—not with the expected rudeness, but with a grace-filled smile that I can never forget. There was no trace of sarcasm or condescension. Is this a small matter? Yes, but I am forever a better driver because of it.

Please discuss the content of the article before considering the Reflection questions, Page 73.

Paul Stimson

Love is Never Having to ... what?

> *Faith, hope and love abide, these three,*
> *and the greatest is love.*
> *(I Corinthians 13:13)*

Some people have earned a place in history by a one-liner. Patrick Henry is famous solely for, "Give me liberty or give me death"[18]; Admiral Farragut for, "Damn the torpedoes; full speed ahead."[19] Others have suffered ridicule in the same manner: Barry Goldwater for, "Extremism in defense of liberty is no vice"[20]; Erich Segal for, "Love is never having to say you're sorry."[21]

This is to suggest that the Segal quote is not wrong-headed: it is just that he did not say enough. An alternate wording might be; An apology spoken through clenched teeth is no apology. Picture a playground scene: Billy's mom arrives just in time to find him fighting with Tommy; she pulls him away and, clamping him between crouched knees, orders "Now tell Tommy you're sorry." Tommy is not fooled by the mumbled apology; there is no repentance and no restoration. The scene is set for the next, more aggravated, round.

Chapter II – Knowledge for the Heart

The Church, in some times and places, has made the same tragic error by making the *Sacrament of Confession* mandatory. Repentance is an act of free will. In our families and friendships, many of us perpetuate the error much of the time by expecting, even demanding, an apology for every wrong. This is the crux of Segal's statement: Love is never having to say you're sorry. That is, never being coerced to say you are sorry.

St. Paul's famous paean to love (I Corinthians 13:4-7), is often quoted but perhaps too seldom contemplated. Please take time for a slow, phrase-by-phrase reading:

Love is patient; love is kind; Love is not envious or boastful or arrogant or rude. It does not insist on its own way; it is not irritable or resentful; It does not rejoice in wrongdoing, but rejoices in the truth. It bears all things, believes all things, hopes all things, endures all things.

Some families read these verses aloud every day. Love that lives by this description says "sorry" readily, painlessly, joyously. It may be spoken without words: a meeting of the eyes, a touch of lips on lips. When the apology is not demanded, the ever-present issue of pride fades a bit.

In verse 8, St. Paul goes on to say: Love never ends. That is a jarring statement in this era of 50% divorce rate. Could love in this pattern ever end? Conversely, if it ends, was it ever love in the first place?

Please discuss the content of the article before considering the Reflection questions, Page 74.

Paul Stimson

Hendrick's Journey[22]
A new twist on an old tale

> *Thus you will know them by their fruits.*
> *(Matthew 7:20)*

Hendrick arrived at the Pearly Gates and was greeted by St. Peter: "Hendrick, do you wish to enter?"

"Well, I'm not sure," quipped Hendrick. "I've a hunch that most of my friends are down in the Other Place."

"Saint or no saint," groaned Peter: "I don't know how I've stood it, hearing the same gag for nigh onto 2000 years—and who knows how many millennia more?

"But I've just figured out how to deal with you incurable jokesters: I shall take you quite literally. Before this day is over you will have seen both options, and the choice will be yours."

Peter led Hendrick first to the Gate of Hell. "Strange," mused Hendrick: "No flames, no pitchfork-wielding demons." Instead, a gray pall of silence.

He could, indeed, recognize the gaunt shells of some of his friends, seated at one great table. Curiouser and curiouser: the odor drifting through the iron bars was not that of sulfurous smoke—it was the tantalizing aroma of delicacies beyond imagining. With

Chapter II – Knowledge for the Heart

eyes adapting to the gloom, he could see that the table was bent under the weight of heavenly foods.

Hendrick sputtered incoherently: "But how in . . . "

"Precisely so," interrupted Peter. "Now look closely."

With pupils fully dilated at last, Hendrick saw that a long spoon was securely attached to each person's hand, and the design of the seating had been carefully planned so that the Damned could reach limitless delicacies but could not get them to their mouths.

"Fiendish, devilish, demonic," exploded Hendrick. I would prefer fire and brimstone any day."

"Any *Eternity,*" corrected Peter. "Now hurry along."

Returning to the Pearly Gates, Hendrick was able to get a closer look inside. Through a blur of bewilderment he grasped the incredible: the table, the heaping platters, the chairs and—how possibly—the long spoons, were identical to those in the scene below! Here, too, he recognized some of his friends: their faces shone.

Heart pounding, he watched as the minuscule difference unfolded: the people, unable to reach their own mouths, had quickly learned that they could reach each other's. The feasting and the merriment seemed endless, and they delighted in choosing the tastiest morsels for each other. Hendrick's knees went wobbly and he sat down clumsily on the lapis lazuli curbstone of the Golden Street. Peter squatted beside him and rested his hand—the weather-beaten hand of an Eternal Fisherman— on his shoulder.

"Small difference," mused Peter. "In fact, Hell was not always shrouded in silence. You see, the Damned are not stupid: they learned just as fast as the Saved that they could reach each others' mouths. But right away there was a complaint of a streak of gristle in a bite of unicorn steak, then another grumbled over a shell fragment in the lobster ambrosia. The din rose, then began the retaliation: Oh, my God what retaliation—smaller bites, heedlessly chosen. Spoons clanging against teeth. The uproar subsided as some stopped feeding each other altogether. Then the maliciousness: I saw one feed another a cocktail frankfurter with the toothpick broken off inside it."

"There is something I am not understanding," said Hendrick, slowly: "I'm thinking down the list of friends I recognized in both places and I don't see the difference. I must apologize for my poor joke when first we met."

"I think I see what is troubling you," said Peter, briskly: "the friends you see below weren't 'bad' and the ones above weren't 'good'. Does that express it compactly?"

"Couldn't have said it better myself," replied Hendrick: "what am I failing to see?"

"People can't see into each other's hearts the way God can," began Peter, quietly: "I vividly remember the way Jesus put it one day: '. . .*Where your treasure is, there will be your heart also.*' By the time he began his ministry, He knew at the core of his being the Truths that the rest of us grasp so gradually, so painfully. Most people *want* to love: it feels good so they seek more. What they

Chapter II – Knowledge for the Heart

miss is that love isn't a feeling, it is a decision: sometimes it doesn't even feel good—at least, not the way we usually seek good feelings. During my last years on Earth I finally learned that I have no ability to love. All I could do was get out of the way and let the love of God shine through me. Much of the 'love' that gets passed around is a poor imitation, which boils down to a kind of self-interest—a bargain or a barter, you might call it. It says, 'I will rub your back because I love the way you rub mine.' But motives matter: the bargain breaks down as people demand ever more and offer ever less."

Hendrick sat in stunned silence. "I know I could have grasped that sooner," he mused at length. "Peter, may I have a last look at my friends below?"

"Surely," said Peter. As they neared the cold, iron gates—ironic iron that can never rust—his voice fell to a whisper: "I remember the day the uproar ended, and only a few angry expletives punctured the silence. The very last sound heard 'round the table was that of an unpalatable mass of gristle being spat back in the face of the one who had proffered it."

Words failed. Ears adapt to silence just as pupils dilate in darkness. Gradually, Hendrick became aware of a steady drip of tears from above as the Host of Heaven wept, punctuated by the spatter of an occasional drop of blood—the Blood of the Paschal Lamb.

Please discuss the content of the article before considering the Reflection questions, Page 74.

Paul Stimson

Forgiveness

> *Remember not the sins of my youth,*
> *or my transgressions.*
> *(Psalm 25:7a)*

The court system dispenses justice, then clears the table so life can go on. But what was on the table sifts into a great filing system, ready to be displayed as a backdrop if ever a repeat case is opened. The files outlive us by decades, even centuries.

Theologians reassure us that the Great Filing-Cabinet-in-the-Sky is not like that. It is a cabinet with no bottom; its contents go into free-fall through all eternity. Through the mystery of Grace, what is forgiven is forgotten, and a new offense is as if committed by a newborn.

But how can this be? Does it mean that our sin doesn't matter? Quite the opposite: sins, great and small, wound God more than we can imagine. But the restoration is forever his first objective, and forgiveness is an essential starting point. Thereafter, remembering our sins would serve no purpose.

This God-like quality does not come readily to us, but we do well to learn it. Human brains have a staggering capacity for long-

Chapter II – Knowledge for the Heart

term memory. I still remember 04SN-71589, the serial number of my first bicycle in 1937. If I tried to force myself to forget these ancient trivia, the effort would only embed them all the more vividly. But I can barely remember what I had for breakfast yesterday, and Monday's breakfast is gone forever. This distinction between long- and short-term memory surely is not accidental, and that distinction can be of value to us.

The cynic says, "Fool me once, shame on you. Fool me twice, shame on me." "Forewarned is forearmed." "I can forgive, but I can never forget." We do scrutinize each other's behavior, watching for patterns. Spoken or not, the reaction to a repeated offense is, "There you go again." Each repetition reinforces the pathway from short- to long-term memory and the filing cabinet bulges.

Expectations have a powerful effect on behavior. The effect is totally automatic. A child receiving an excellent report is motivated to earn another; a poor report evokes, "Why bother?" When I sense a "There you go again," self-improvement is farthest from my mind.

But suppose, just suppose for a moment, that we did come up with a Godlike ability and willingness to wipe the slate clean. Then the next repetition of my besetting sin would evoke a startled look, and "Why, Sweetheart, where did that come from? That's not like you!" Would not the downward spiral end there and then?

Long-term memory is formed in proportion to the emotional impact of the event. If the offended party can lighten-up just a little, maybe with a humorous twist, the stress level will ease and maybe the trauma will not be etched quite so deeply into memory. It takes practice; gradually we can learn not to sweat the small stuff, and the relationship thrives proportionately—if, and only if, it is on a two-way path. Grace and justice are ever in tension; love withers when the beloved remains beyond reach.

Please discuss the content of the article before considering the Reflection questions, Page 75.

Chapter II – Knowledge for the Heart

Fear & Fear

> *...I will fear no evil, for thou art with me.*
> *(Psalm 23:4)*
> *Ye that fear the Lord, praise him.*
> *(Psalm 22:23)*

Many of the essays of this series are headed by two contrasting words: Light & Darkness, Scarcity & Abundance, etc. But Fear & Fear?

Yes, fear and fear. The English language is in most respects the richest in all history, affording shades of meaning as no other. Languages spawn fine distinctions in matters that people are attentive to; I have heard that the Eskimos have fifty different words for snow. The Greeks had four words for love, and I can find eight in Hebrew. Perhaps it is significant that English lumps them all into one.

Similarly, we use fear for two vastly different feelings and thus blur the distinction between them. We fear all the dangers of the world around us and try to build walls of security, ignoring God's insistent plea that we " . . . fear no evil." Ultimately, if we look deep inside, most of us most of the time fear damnation. In response, we tend toward frenzied bursts of self-improvement, best seen in the prodding of children to "be good" as Christmas approaches. Between times, we tend to slump into a kind of hopeless resignation that it won't work: We tell ourselves that there is no amount of "shaping up" that will earn a passing grade, so why try?

That conclusion is correct, of course, but it is right for a reason directly opposite our own. When will we learn that God's acceptance of us, who we are and as we are, is total, unquestioning, unconditional? By scaling that cliff, which rises into the Valley of the Shadow of Death, we arrive at a place in which we can, for the first time, enter into the Fear of the Lord . . . the beginning of Wisdom. (Psalm 111:10). We would do ourselves (and the English Language) an everlasting favor if we would learn to call it awe, thus distinguishing it from our mortal terrors, which are Satan's favorite hunting ground.

We hesitate to enter wholeheartedly into the awe of the Lord because, in the kernel of our being, we are programmed to "be big," and to compete vigorously with any threat to our bigness. What we in our worm's-eye view fail to grasp is that we have only to step back and leave to God the infinite bigness which is uniquely his. (Sounds easy, doesn't it?) Wonder of wonders, we are thus drawn into that bigness, and find ourselves far greater than anything we could pump ourselves up to. The Great History Book in the Sky ranks as least all those who have striven for greatness.

Fear casts out love, as surely as love casts out fear. Resurrected out of our fear, we are free to be drawn into the awe of the Lord. In

Chapter II – Knowledge for the Heart

the Letter to the Romans Paul, after seven chapters of wrestling with the self-defeating aspects of the human condition, leads off Chapter Eight with a startling shift of wind: There is, therefore, now no condemnation for those who are in Christ Jesus.

Fear might have its place in the Spiritual Journey: it might be the one force for jolting a person out of an unexamined life. In the next step, the need is seen to " . . . work out [their] salvation in fear and trembling." Then let fear be banished so we may live in . . . awe and trembling. Fear impels us toward flight or denial; awe draws us to intimacy and worship. We may in time discover that awe is a force that cuts deeper even than fear.

Please discuss the content of the article before considering the Reflection questions, Page 75.

Paul Stimson

Belonging & Longing

> *As the deer longs for the water-brooks, so longs my soul for you, O God. My soul is athirst for God, athirst for the living God; when shall I come to appear before the presence of God?*
> *(Psalm 42, 1 –2)*

A clergyman once baptized his own granddaughter. In his sermon, he spoke touchingly of our being baptized not only into belonging but also into longing.

The Kingdom of Heaven is, first and foremost, a love affair—and what lover fails to long for the beloved? The Kingdom of Heaven is not just pie in the sky; it is here and now; it is in the midst of us (Luke 17:21). If love were (as is widely believed) just a feeling, we would be off the hook: we could claim that it's not our fault when it comes and goes.

But love is a decision; it is also a commandment, . . .*that you love one another; even as I have loved you, that you also love one another.* (John 13:34). Pray that simple obedience to that

Chapter II – Knowledge for the Heart

command will wash away all the "shoulds and oughts" which becloud our longing.

Please discuss the content of the article before considering the Reflection questions, Page 76..

Paul Stimson

Gratitude

...Take what he gives/ And praise him still, Through good or ill,/ Who ever lives! (Richard Baxter)[23]

We have all been taught manners: we say, "thank you" when a gift is offered. The gratitude bursts through when the gift is pleasing; when not, we try to cover a disappointment with politeness, yet knowing that the faint smile will be noticed, and will make it known that we didn't need another pair of socks.

What a blessing that we can dare to be more real with God! Unhesitatingly, we grumble at him when we don't like the latest turn of events. In the worst of times, hot anger may erupt.

Rejoice that God is not fickle.

Abraham Lincoln[24] was asked (in the worst of times) whether he believed that God is on our side. He replied that God may have purposes beyond either ours or the other's side. Surely Joseph didn't think it was one of his better days when his brothers cast him into a pit and sold him to passing gypsies.

Years later, he and they alike saw it as the key to saving God's Chosen People from the famine. (Genesis 50:15 –21)

Chapter II – Knowledge for the Heart

Henri Nouwen[25] wrote: *Gratitude . . . is a response to grace. The compassionate life is a grateful life, and actions born out of gratefulness are not compulsive but free, not somber but joyful, not fanatical but liberating. When gratitude is the source of our actions, our giving becomes receiving and those to whom we minister become our ministers.*

God can and will bring good out of anything and everything—things we embrace and things we hate or dread. We are free to be grateful or petulant, meaning that we will either assist or obstruct the coming of the Kingdom.

Please discuss the content of the article before considering the Reflection questions, Page 76.

Paul Stimson

Meatballs

He has put down the mighty from their seat, and exalted the humble and meek.
(Luke 1:52)

It seems that every generation has its own streak of goofiness: in the 1920s people filled the air with *23 Skidoo*, long past the time when anyone remembered what it meant. Decades later, *See ya later, alligator* evoked the response, *In a while, crocodile*. Mindless but harmless.

In the bleak 1930s, somehow *Shoot the sherbet to me, Herbert* gave rise to the response, *Shoot the meatballs to me, Dominick*, making no sense at all. Predictably, one publicity-hound assembled half a roomful of Herberts armed with sherbet, then the other side with meatball-laden Dominicks. The instruction was, of course, that, on a cue, the participants would shout the above clichés, then let fly while the instigator captured the event on movie film.

Maybe he was too busy with aiming limelights and setting exposure; notice the buzz in the air and a few Doms and Herbs slipping forth into 'enemy' territory. When he rolled the film and

Chapter II – Knowledge for the Heart

gave the cue they all turned on him, burying him and his camera in meatballs and sherbet.

My hunch is that, in most times and places, his scheme would have worked as planned. Adolph Hitler had just demonstrated how easy it was to get people marching in lockstep, singing *Deutschland über Alles* and ratting to the Gestapo about any dissidents in their midst. When the human spirit is depressed, people have trouble seeing the larger picture, and can even be induced to vote against their own best interests.

We live in a culture which has for many generations valued rote learning above critical thinking. So it comes to pass that the corrupting influence of money in campaign politics, long a problem, is only now beginning to attract some overdue attention as their influence peddling which was once subtle has become blatant.

The forcing function is, obviously, the enormous cost of television air- time, which has proved to be the most effective way of reaching the most people.

It all works as it does for one simple mindless reason: relentless, repetitive exposure is evidently more persuasive than meaningful content. Lost on the masses is one not-so-challenging bit of logic: that the side making more noise has raised more money, thus is predictably the more corrupted by special interests. The wake-up call is as easy as sherbet and meatballs: reformers have only to publicize the totals, urging people to vote against the bigger fund-raisers — enlightened self-interest in its simplest form.

Paul Stimson

In laboratory experiments, people tend to behave like laboratory rats, emitting programmed responses, unless someone reminds them that they are deciders, equipped with minds that can question. When we become self-aware we stop behaving like laboratory rats and become human, in the image of God—or, at least, aware that bombarding the photographer is an option.

Races are getting tighter: influencing even a small number of voters with this simple logic would soon have a visible effect. Lewis Carroll would have loved the next scene, with campaign managers vying to raise less money than the opposition.

Think about it, Dom and Herb: no joke here, because it could work.

Please discuss the content of the article before considering the Reflection questions, Page 76.

Reflection Questions - Chapter II

Free Will

1) What battles in your life could you win simply by surrendering?
2) In what ways are you enslaved by your fears?
3) If you have now, or ever have had a pet, in what ways has the pet's love outshone yours?
4) Ponder the concept of *Fear of the Lord*. Which is uppermost in your mind: fear or awe?
5) Do you ever think that you would rather be an ant or a bee, rather than human?
6) Pondering the concept of *God making us in his own image*: what elements of that image make us uniquely human, in contrast with the other animals?
7) Does the possibility of being abandoned by God strike fear into your heart? If so, does that put you into a scramble to 'shape up?' If so, can you pause a moment and consider that you might have it exactly backwards?

Light & Darkness

1) Give examples of darkness as a positive thing: i. e. "Under the shadow of his wing," a good night's sleep.

2) When was the last time you spent time with God in the darkness?
3) Distinguish between the darkness of despair and the darkness of refreshment and intimacy.
4) Try closing your eyes to close out the din of the world, and hear God's "Still, small voice."

Suffering

1) Have you faced a time of suffering that made you stronger or more compassionate?
2) How has God used your suffering to help others?
3) If suffering were God's punishment, how could we account for Christ suffering?
4) A Holy Week prayer: "...that we, walking in the way of the cross, may find it none other than the way of life and peace"

Amphetamines, Narcotics & Endorphins

1) Have you ever experienced the rush of endorphins? The runner's high? The rush of peace that comes with laughter or being loved?
2) What spiritual exercises might you take on to build your "faith endorphins?"
3) Where do you most often find laughter?
4) Do you know people who exude a sense of peace or serenity?

Chapter II – Knowledge for the Heart

5) What can you say to a person who obsesses or struggles with things that cannot be changed?

Trust & Trustworthiness

1) Have you ever offered your trust to one whose trustworthiness was in doubt?
2) How did the outcome, positive or negative, impact you?
3) What kind of a God can say, "There is joy in the presence of the angels of God over one sinner who repents?"

The Judas Syndrome

1) Are you brave enough to be honest with God?
2) Are you comfortable in familiar ruts? Or do you welcome missteps, however painful, knowing they may enhance your understanding of God?
3) How would you personally define "courageous love"?
4) What helps us develop the ability to love courageously?

Anger Management

1) How readily do you anger? How do you express your anger?
2) Were you aware of psychology's four basic emotions? (A chart of the four basic emotions can be viewed at *http://www.psychologyofmen.org/index.php?itemid=35*)

3) It has been said that anger rides on a sea of fear. Can you see fear in your anger?
4) What anger-management techniques do you use?
5) List the things that anger you the most.
    a) Are these constructive or destructive anger?
    b) What would turn destructive angers into "noble" anger?
6) Have you experienced mindlessly evil people?
7) Can you leave vengeance to God? Why or why not?

Love Is Never Having to... What?

1) Does *I Corinthians 13* apply to all types of love (filial, eros, charity, agape)? Why?
2) Is love enough? What other qualities are needed in relationships?
3) Sometimes it's a real puzzlement to figure out what we did for which we're supposed to be sorry. Why?
4) Why do marriages die?

Hendrick's Journey

1. To whom do you need to reach out?
2. What stands in the way of letting God shine through you?
3. Does your God consign the lost to Hell for breaking his commandments?

Chapter II – Knowledge for the Heart

4. Does your God weep for his children who are lost to his love?
5. If you had a child who had "gone bad," what would you do? Take into account factors like anger and hurt, reaching out or condemning, free will and the disciplining of the willful.

Forgiveness

1) What happens to a child (or even an adult) when we constantly rub their noses in what they have done wrong?
2) What happens to a child when a mother or father says, "I forgive you" and hugs him/her in her arms with love?
3) Can we grow into a loving person without having experienced loving forgiveness along the way?
4) What does God want us to become?
5) What is your best defense against sin? Is it self-image: I don't want to be that kind of person. Or do you see sin for what it is in God's eyes: simply a violation of Love?

Fear & Fear

1) A chart of the four basic emotions can be viewed at *http://www.psychologyofmen.org/index.php?itemid=35*
2) How strong is your self-improvement resolve? What gets in the way of success?
3) When was the last time you were awed by or feared God?
4) What synonyms would you use for "being big" in your eyes? In God's eyes?

5) How does the modern Church promote fear?
6) Why does the modern Church promote fear?
7) How have you seen God break the bonds of fear and encourage awe?

Belonging & Longing

1) What gets in the way of your sense of belonging?
2) What gets in the way of your sense of longing?
3) Have you ever heard a friend express an emptiness or longing for belonging?
4) How do you experience the presence of the Holy One?

Gratitude

1) Think of an occasion when your 'worst of times' ended up blessing you.
2) How can you hold onto that understanding when future 'worst times' occur?
3) When the Drill Instructor assigns you twenty push-ups, are you willing to shoot back the proper answer, which is "Thank you sir. And may I have twenty more?"

Meatballs

1) What special-interest groups give you most cause for concern?
2) What spiritual slogans have meaning for you?
3) How can we escape mindless passivity?

Chapter II – Knowledge for the Heart

4) Surely it is easier to train children to behave and conform, than to consider and choose. Ponder the consequences.

Chapter III – Knowledge for the Soul

The locus of the Soul is less clearly defined: it just feels like it is somewhere deeper inside. We do well to turn to poetry:

And so the yearning strong,
With which the soul will long,
shall far outpass the power of human telling;
for none can guess its grace,
till Love create a place
wherein the Holy Spirit makes a dwelling.
~Bianco da Siena (d. 1434?)

Chapter III – Knowledge for the Soul

Evil

> *An enemy has done this.*
> *(Matthew 13:28)*

You might be puzzled to see a chapter on feeding the soul lead off with such a jarring title. But the soul is not just a warm, fuzzy place; it is the armory of our battle against the forces of evil. Some may say, "Pooh, pooh; there is no evil." To this I reply that unbelief is Satan's favorite hiding place.

A principle in Zen philosophy states that nothing exists without its opposite. Pondering this brought to mind my earliest episode of real, experiential learning. When I was very young my parents somehow got the idea that unless pressured, I would not eat enough. Having choked down more food than I needed at one meal, I was not hungry for the next. I can recall being puzzled at hearing people say they were hungry yet not having, until years later, any clue to what they were feeling.

So it is that goodness would have no meaning in a world devoid of evil.

But isn't evil simply something that we do on our own, or slip into by failing to do good? Once again I suggest that Satan would like to have us see it that way. But the scriptural recounting of the temptation of Jesus by Satan in the wilderness, reported in the Gospels of Matthew (4:1 11), Mark (1:12 13) and Luke (4:113) conceives evil as a personal will, openly and actively hostile to God. C. S. Lewis expands on this theme in his novel, The Screwtape Letters, in which an evil middle manager named Screwtape issues intricate and exhaustive instruction to an underling, Wormwood, on the weakness and gullibility of the human soul.

How is it that Jesus, noted as being. fully human as we are, (Hebrews 2:17 18) was able to resist Satan's delectable temptations? My take is that his intimate connection to God the Father was so complete that the desire not to sin trumped the powerful urges. Stated another way, the motivation was love, not fear of consequences. So let it be with us.

Since Jesus did not yield, the power of Satan was nil. James (4:7) avers, "Resist the devil and he will flee from you." But, just as a soft spot in the levee leads to a flood, sin, even "small" sin, is an invitation to the Evil One and all his forces. He is able to lead us beyond where we thought we wanted to go.

So, maybe this is something Christians need to wrestle with, but how is it a concern for non-believers? Surely Satan need not bother with them, for they are already in his pocket.

Please discuss the content of the article before considering the Reflection questions, Page 130.

Chapter III – Knowledge for the Soul

The Power of Satan

Almighty God, unto whom all hearts are open, all desires known, and from whom no secrets are hid...
(The Collect for Purity)

It is well established that Satan has no power over anyone unless invited in. "Resist the devil and he will flee from you," says the Letter of James (4:7b). The verse makes it sound so maddeningly simple, 'though it is frustratingly difficult. I am glad God understands that "we are but dust." (Psalm 103:14b). It makes us squirm and we like to joke about it: "I can resist anything but temptation" is a favorite quip of mine.

Satan knows better than to put before us a direct temptation to sin. Our pride, our Puritan rectitude would be enough to keep us on the straight and narrow. But aah, to pose something better than God's best — that is a lode worth mining. That was the serpent's ploy in the Garden of Eden (Genesis 3), and it has been working ever since.

Sins of action and inaction capture most of our attention most of time. Satan thinks that is just fine; he enjoys disrupting our actions and interactions, and is happy to keep us distracted from matters of inner being where he can do the most harm. Psalm 51:6 reads:

"Behold, thou desirest truth in the inward being; therefore teach me wisdom in my secret heart."

My natural tendency is to keep my prayer life in one compartment and my approach to practical matters of life in another. If there are serious issues I usually manage to invite God in; I hope I will live long enough to combine those two compartments into one. Br. Curtis Almquist, SSJE wrote: "*The early desert monastics learned what is repeated again and again in the wisdom literature of the Scriptures: you cannot do it alone. Left alone, to our own devices, cleverness, and calculations, we are incredibly vulnerable to self-deception.*"

In the spiritual domain there is no neutral territory: We resist temptation or we yield to it; we repent or go our defiant way. That which we do not deed to God is Satan's by default. And diabolically clever is an inadequate description of his way. He will not let up; he will take us places we could not have imagined.

But take heart: this side of the grave, Satan has no permanent victories.

Please discuss the content of the article before considering the Reflection questions, Page 130.

Chapter III – Knowledge for the Soul

The Will of God

> *But to all who received him, who believed in his name, he gave power to become children of God*
> *(John 1:12)*

There has been more hokum written about the will of God than about perhaps any other subject, with the possible exception of sex. I am trying to overcome the prevailing notion that the will of God is like a railroad track laid before us[26], so that we are at all times either on or off that track. (If that were the design, I am sure that we would all be off the track all the time.) The railroad-track conception demands that we look ahead to see where we are going. When we think we understand his will at one level, we can be sure we are missing the point at numerous other levels! If we must think in terms of railroad tracks, the better perspective is that if we look behind we see track, but none before us.

Once again I am indebted to my father for a fitting parable: the rug makers of old Persia, world-famous for their rich colors and textures and for their intricate designs (no two alike, ever) functioned as a family business. At the start of a new rug the backing was hung from the ceiling by one edge, so it divided the room in two. The family with dyed yarns gathered on one side, while the patriarch sat alone on the other. By an intricate series of commands, the patriarch called out what colors were to go in which positions. The workers could see a little of the emerging pattern but only from the rather lifeless back side. Only the patriarch could see the whole pattern in all its richness of texture.

Knotting yarns is tedious work. Most workers got bored or distracted with thoughts of next Saturday's date; at times some became angry or spiteful and deliberately put in wrong colors. The patriarch had long since learned that if he stopped to correct mistakes the rug would never get done and they would all starve. Therefore, he never broke stride in the stream of commands; instead he noted each error, and in his mind he redesigned the pattern to incorporate it. No rug of such intricate beauty could have ever been made by any other means.

Thus we see that the all-powerful God once again confronts us with a paradox, in that he who created all things and wrote all the rules, who could make us do absolutely everything "by the numbers," chose from the beginning to surrender that will, leaving us free to accept or to reject—to love or to perish. No god conjured up in our collective imagination has ever done that.

Am I saying that God, having surrendered his will, no longer has a will? Certainly not: the message we are asked to get through our skulls is that the surrendered will is the perfected will—be it God's or ours. Like any good military commander, God absolutely never asks of us anything he himself is unwilling to do. The anonymous classic, The Cloud of Unknowing[27] tells us that foresight is precisely the thing that the Spiritual Journey does not provide. John Henry Newman conveyed the same in his great hymn[28]:

Lead kindly light amid the encircling gloom,
Lead thou me on:
The night is dark and I am far from home:
Lead thou me on.
Guide thou my feet: I cannot hope to see
The distant scene, one step enough for me.

The late Bishop Stephen Bayne[29] wrote: *God put freedom into his created universe in order that the universe could respond to his love with an answering love of its own . . . He put into the created universe a principle of choice, and he paid a twofold price for that. First, he limited his own freedom to have everything his own way, Second, he committed himself to having to win out of freedom what he could have perfectly easily commanded as a right.*

Please discuss the content of the article before considering the Reflection questions, Page 131.

Paul Stimson

Judgment Day

> *Oh, you can't get to Heaven in powder and paint,*
> *'Cause the Lord don't want you as you ain't.*
> *I ain't gonna grieve my Lord no more!*
> *(Traditional)*

The concept of an afterlife is a near-universal element in the human view of life and death. It is prominent in most cultures, and no one knows where or when it began. Some have foreseen afterlife as a shadowy semi-consciousness; others as everlasting festivity. It is clearly seen in ancient burial sites, many of them more a preparation for a journey than mere disposal of remains.. These beliefs are deeply embedded in many cultures that could not possibly have communicated with each other; they therefore are perhaps best understood as spiritual knowledge. It is also in many cases understood that not everyone gets there — some winnowing event must be traversed

What kind of a winnowing event? We can only guess, and that guess is usually rooted in dread. It seems likely that the inner knowledge of standards of conduct — and our universal failure to live up to them — goes back to the beginnings of human consciousness. And it is not just human: our domestic animals can

Chapter III – Knowledge for the Soul

and do imitate us. Decades ago we had a collie with a passion for digging in wastebaskets. She knew she could not get away with it when we were home, so preparation for going out included putting all wastebaskets out of reach. Tail high and wagging, she joyously greeted our return. But, if we forgot even one basket we knew it instantly, because she came to the door with head low and tail between her legs. Scolding words were delivered in mock sternness in the midst of a hug, and it seemed she understood the interweaving of love and disapproval.

But, never did she show any sign of changing her ways. Here we can uncover a vital insight, that at some point in human evolution, we became aware that we have some measure of freedom to choose our behavior, and life is better when we are open to changing our ways. This was the dawning of spiritual awareness, preparing us for knowledge and love of God

The opening verses of Genesis deliver to us a shimmering concept: God made us in his own image! But from long before the words of Genesis were written into history, we have been returning the favor — making God in our own image. Deep down we know how wrong this is, and fear warps our behavior. All too often, raw emotions lead to savage actions. When children misbehave, the near-universal impulse — now as well as way back then — is to smack them. Punishing parent automatically leads to the concept of punishing God — an overarching theme in the Hebrew Scriptures, called the Old Testament by Christians.

But it is not all that way; we have only to look more closely. Isaiah's concept of the Suffering Servant is perhaps the greatest breakthrough in the evolution of our concept of the Nature of God. This is clear revelation that God made us in his own image for the purpose of loving us. A loving parent is able to scold misbehavior in a way that builds relationship, rather than tearing it down. And, but for the urge toward relationship, God might not be upset by our behavior.

But our misbehavior causes pain, to ourselves as well as to each other and to God. Pain is a motivating force, and most people will seek escape from it. Anesthetizing it in drugs or alcohol is a downward spiral; people who have built some emotional and spiritual maturity will ponder the cause and seek a healthy solution.

But our culture likes the easy way. As Christmas approaches, we hear words attributed to Santa Claus — and we think Santa is embarrassed to hear it:

He knows when you've been sleeping;

He knows when you are awake.

He knows when you've been bad or good,

So be good, for goodness sake.

And the Latin Requiem Mass is rife with lines that try to scare us into changing our behavior.

Day of vengeance, Day of burning . . .

Deliver me from the mouth of the lion . . .

Liberate me, God, from eternal death in that terrible day. . .

Chapter III – Knowledge for the Soul

What is missing is the realization that behavior is almost immaterial; Only motivation counts. If I do a "good" thing for the more-or-less concealed purpose of my own gain, I have lost it. Better far to have stayed in bed that day.

A Sufi Mystic nailed it with these simple verses:

O my Lord, if I worship you from fear of hellfire,
Burn me in Hell.
If I worship you from hope of Paradise,
Bar me from its gates.
But if I worship you for yourself alone,
Grant me the beauty of your face.

My growing concept of the Day of Judgment steers away from all images of God as a robed judge on a throne, sternly weighing my pluses against my minuses. Rather, I imagine a wordless process, in which my understanding and embrace of the judgment are given highest priority. I imagine myself entering into a whiteness so much whiter than any whiteness I could ever have envisioned, and suddenly seeing myself, my beliefs, my attitudes, my behaviors, starkly contrasted against that withering whiteness. It is the Refiner's Fire, the Fuller's Soap. The dramatic intensity calls to mind the Old Testament Book of Job, in which our hero, after long tribulation, finds himself in the Splendor and Majesty of the Presence of God. All he can find to say is, "I repent in dust and ashes." And here a paradox: repentance surrounded by total love is uplifting, not degrading. A voice resounds — not in English, of course, but in a language I have never heard yet instantly understand: "Enter into the Joy of the Lord."

But the very act of daring to enter into that overwhelming whiteness says something about me. I believe that not all would cross that threshold. Is it possible that those who don't, simply wouldn't like Heaven?

The alternative? The most popular image of Hell is shrouded in fire and brimstone, but might it be more like Narnia, where it is always winter but never Christmas?

Please discuss the content of the article before considering the Reflection questions, Page 131.

Chapter III – Knowledge for the Soul

Was Jesus Christ sinless?

> *For we have not a high priest who is unable to sympathize with our weaknesses, but one who in every respect has been tempted as we are, yet without sin.*
> *(Hebrews 4:15)*

The verse quoted above is one of many that point to an inescapable conclusion: Jesus Christ was fully tempted as we are, yet did not sin. Still, there are some among us who sincerely, even passionately, believe that this could not be. Their reasoning, if I understand it, is that Jesus, in addition to being the fully divine Savior of the World, was also fully human as we are. So, since we all sin, he could not have experienced life as we do, unless sinning as we do.

Following this logic, would one who intends to counsel prisoners on Death Row have to go out and kill someone, in preparation? Or would a student in Dental School have to let her teeth rot? One might hope that these analogies would be enough to flush out the faulty reasoning, but they probably won't, so we will have to explore greater depths.

The key line is, '. . .fully tempted, as we are,' and that thought needs to be unpacked. A comedian once quipped, "I can resist anything but temptation." And my father, a holy man indeed, remarked near the end of his life, "If there is any sin I have never committed, it was because I wasn't seriously tempted, or was too afraid of the consequences." Yes, there are notable exceptions in the midst of us, but the jarring fact is that most of us, most of the time, are inept warriors on Satan's battlefield. And the truth of that conclusion comes into sharper focus if we include Scripture's insight that one who lusts has committed adultery already[30]. That principle extends beyond sexual sin; the object of out-of-control desire might be nothing more compelling than an ice-cream cone.

It has been said that Satan does not waste his energies on those of us who yield without much of a fight. To gain a glimpse of the potential intensity of temptation, think of something you most love to own or love to do, and ponder what it would be like to renounce it for the rest of your days. You might well decide that you couldn't bring yourself to do it, and you might be correct. That is why twelve-step self-help groups urge taking one day at a time; in so doing they call upon spiritual forces that are beyond their reach as individuals.

What is our motive for resisting temptation? It could be pride; we could find ourselves saying, "I do not want to be that kind of person." That was, in fact, the motive of the Pharisees, and the reason Jesus was so down on them. Doing the right things for the wrong reasons left them spiritually worse off than those who never thought about right and wrong. Or the motive could be fear — fear of being condemned on the Day of Judgment. That was the motive of the man who hid his ten talents instead of investing them, and — guess what — his fear earned him the condemnation that he feared[31]. That leaves love, the only worthy motive. If sin is resisted by pride or fear, the cure might be worse than the disease.

To consider how Jesus could have resisted all sin, let us see what his motives might have been. It could not have been fear of the consequences, for he said that perfect love casts out fear. It could not have been pride, for pride is itself the cardinal sin. That leaves only love. He lived 24/7 in perfect Union with God the Father; sin is, first and foremost, the great destroyer of relationship, so that perfect Union could never have taken root if impeded by sin. However compelling a sinful urge might have been, the loving urge was ever stronger.

Finally, let us recall God's motive in sending his Son: it was for the expressed purpose of saving sinners. That goal could have been pursued only by a perfect role model; Jesus could never have been put in the position of saying, lamely, "Do as I say, don't do as I do."

Please discuss the content of the article before considering the Reflection questions, Page 131..

Paul Stimson

Incarnation

> *Lo! he comes with clouds descending,*
> *Once for our salvation slain.*
> *(Charles Wesley)[32]*

Advent is a Mystery: it is a season of looking forward to an already present Reality—the coming of the Christ. As Christians we must learn to live in this paradoxical sense of already-but-not-yet.

What do we mean when we speak of mystery? The first thing to mind, of course, is a detective novel, in which we strive mightily to figure out whodunit, yet secretly hope we have guessed wrong, so we can be surprised on the last page. But in Christian theology, Mystery is not like that: we are called to live in a Reality we will not comprehend this side of Heaven.

What kind of a god would send his only son to dwell among us and (quite predictably) to be murdered by us? In pondering that question we must bear in mind that the concept of capital-G God came quite late in human evolution, and came first to a small, persecuted segment of humankind. There is evidence that prehistoric man knew himself to be a created being, and that creation implies a creator. Our inborn curiosity drives us to

Chapter III – Knowledge for the Soul

contemplate things unknown; surely, a lot of mental energy went into envisioning the nature of the creator. They (like us, their descendants) would start with what they knew and work toward the unknown. The automatic question is: "If I were the creator, what would I be like?" They—being fallen creatures like us—would conceive a tyrant god, designing a creation to serve his every need, every whim. Every pagan god conceived by the mind of man has had this self-serving nature. The pagan gods have never asked to be loved. To quote a cynic, "God created man in his own image and man returned the compliment."

Let us not lose sight: however faulty their vision, their motives were worthy. They wanted to know their creator. God saw that they weren't about to "get it," so chose Israel to hear new, intensely personal revelation. This is the starting point of our journey.

It seems that many of us Christians are still stuck in the pagan vision of God as a tyrant, demanding much and giving little. The concept of fear of the Lord is deeply misunderstood; we might begin to grasp it if we called it awe of the Lord. God's motives are so, so different from our own: He simply loves us, asking only that we respond to that love.

It seems a small thing, compared to a pagan god's demand for human sacrifice. The rapid conversion of Mexico is partly the result of the Aztec gods demanding human sacrifices, compared to the Christian God who sent his only Son to be the sacrifice for our Salvation.

The fact is that this simple act of love "...*demands my soul my life, my all.*" (Isaac Watts)[33]. Thanks be to God, who will wait while we creep toward him, an inch at a time.

O come let us adore him.

Please discuss the content of the article before considering the Reflection questions, Page 132.

Chapter III – Knowledge for the Soul

Faith

Lord, I believe; help my unbelief.
(Mark 9:24)

The Baltimore journalist H. L. Mencken[34], perhaps the most caustic of all unbelievers, wrote: "Faith may be defined briefly as an illogical belief in the occurrence of the improbable." I, an ordinary church-going Christian, do not dispute his words, except that my definition of illogical differs from his: I see God as not illogical, but as transcending logic. Mencken might not have even attempted to grasp that idea. Consider an analogy: primitive peoples didn't know why the sun rises, and lived in fear that it would fail them some day. To introduce them to the simple, logical mechanics of the Solar System would demand a stretch that some of them might be unwilling to attempt.

At the opposite pole, the Bible-thumping fundamentalist is, in my opinion, just as far from faith as was Mencken. Both fail to appreciate the subtlety, the complexity, the untidiness, the Mystery and the paradox of life, love and the universe.

Between that rock (scornful disbelief) and that hard place (rigid literalism) lies the Narrow Gate, which leads to the Fertile Crescent of faith. The famed jurist Billings Learned Hand wrote: "The spirit of liberty is the spirit which is not too sure that it is right." Similarly, faith and doubt are constant companions. First we take baby steps; in time we . . . *walk by faith, not by sight. (II Corinthians 5:7).*

Please discuss the content of the article before considering the Reflection questions, Page 132.

Chapter III – Knowledge for the Soul

Predestination

> *However, no one knows the day or hour when these things will happen, not even the angels in heaven or the Son himself. Only the Father knows.*
> *(Mark 13:32)*

This is to suggest that there is a sense in which the concept of Predestination is sound theology. But that sense is far removed from the tortured reasoning of John Calvin and his followers, now largely abandoned in the Churches. It is farther still from the popular understanding, which interprets it as, "Why bother, because we are all saved or damned no matter what."

All thought systems are grounded in some set of assumptions about the nature of Reality. I see two possible foundations for Predestination: one in which some people are well made of good stuff that will make the grade on Judgment Day, and others not. The other possible foundation is simply capriciousness and randomness. The heathen gods, unloving and not asking to be loved, might conceive such approaches. Even Yahweh of the Old Testament is seen by some as capable of such actions.

But Jesus came to tell us that God is not like that. The letters of John tell us in impassioned terms that God is Love; it is clear that no unloving action could stem from God. In the words of Isaiah (42:3): A bruised reed will he not break, and a dimly burning wick will he not quench. Salvation is freely offered to all; we are free to accept or reject.

So, how do we find a foundation for Predestination in this? Let us ponder Eternity, which many people see as an indefinitely long time, but is better thought of as somehow beyond space and time. Surely God is not traveling through time with us and wondering what will happen next. I envision Eternity as an eternal now in which all of space and time can be viewed as one vast panorama, in which all we have thought, said and done, and all we will think, say and do, form the total reality of our lives. Viewed from our Journey it appears to be open-ended, and it really is: we have not yet made all our decisions. But viewed in Eternity there is no was, is and will be; there is simply now, even though in the world of space and time we did, we do, we will do. It all mattered, matters, will matter.

Please discuss the content of the article before considering the Reflection questions, Page 132.

Chapter III – Knowledge for the Soul

Vulnerability

> *For whoever would save his life will lose it . . .*
> *(Mark 8:35a)*

A primitive organism, drifting in the warm, primordial sea, chanced upon a fragment of calcium. Finding it hard and tasteless, the creature spat it out, thus becoming the ancestor of all jellyfish. Soon another tasted the calcium, and thought it marvelous: gathering all it could find, it built a shell around itself, thus becoming the ancestor of all shellfish, tortoises and armadillos. A third creature, watching all this, understood the qualities of calcium but decided to take it inside, building instead of a shell, a spine. This, the ancestor of all of us, was unwilling to trade away swiftness, gracefulness and its soft, feeling exterior, for mere safety[35].

The price of security is isolation. Clams and oysters can't comprehend this, for they cannot imagine life outside the shell. But if you wander into a stand of marsh grasses, any red-winged blackbird will risk its personal safety to squall out a warning to the community. The paradox is that when each member takes a relatively small risk, the community as a whole becomes much safer—and that includes, of course, each-and-every risk-taker!. We are witnessing the same in the vulnerable heroes of our time. When Nazi forces occupied tiny, vulnerable Denmark, they ordered (as they had elsewhere) that all Jews wear a yellow Star of David. Next morning the King of Denmark wore a yellow star, and his subjects followed suit. The deportation plan of the Nazis was thus thwarted[36].

John Mogabgab[37] once invited participants in a workshop to voice their associations with the word vulnerability. Responses included words such as meek, intimidated, naive and inferior. Vulnerability is seen as a weakness to be overcome, and we base our strategies and policies, both personal and national, on security. What we seek is invulnerability, which can never be attained. Thus we work against one of our deepest needs, the community, closeness, intimacy, which are attainable only through the melting down of the walls of self-protection.

What we are failing to grasp is that there are two distinct types of vulnerability, and the passive type imprisons us by default if we fail to choose the active type. We were made to be vulnerable. God, who has the power to be completely self-protective, chooses to be vulnerable—and he made us in his own image. Jesus faced the choice at every step; when the forces of darkness were closing in on him in the Garden of Gethsemane, he said: *Do you think that I cannot appeal to my Father, and he will at once send me more than twelve legions of angels? (Matthew 26:53).*

We could go on at some length about great people facing world-changing crises, but what about ordinary people in ordinary crises?

Chapter III – Knowledge for the Soul

The rude shock is that there is no difference. These great ones had patterned their responses through small and mid-sized challenges, winning some and losing some, just like the rest of us. What these greats have in common is that they knew better than to rely on their own strength, courage and wisdom. They also knew that their mortal lives were at stake, but accepted that reality.

Elton Trueblood[38] observed that courage is the primary virtue, because all the other virtues presuppose it.

So, biggest of all are the things which seem smallest of all: our almost-automatic ways of masking our true selves, camouflaging our vulnerabilities. "A strong offense is the best defense," we are told, as we sink deeper into isolation. Hell scarcely needs to have a location in celestial geography: we build so many personal hells-on-earth.

Please discuss the content of the article before considering the Reflection questions, Page 133.

Paul Stimson

Worthiness

> *Lord, I am not worthy that Thou shouldst come under my roof, but speak the word only and thy servant shall be healed.*
> *(Matthew 8:8)*
> *. .asking that you may be filled with the knowledge of his will in all spiritual wisdom and understanding, to lead a life worthy of the Lord . . .*
> *(Colossians 1:9–10)*

There is a legend of ancient China, in which a rare species of fish was highly prized, and served only to selected guests on special occasions. These self-effacing guests deemed themselves unworthy of this honor, and the prized platter passed around the table, untouched. We can be sure that the 'leftovers' were not discarded; thus we see the irony that only the servants proved to be 'worthy'. (The legend goes on to say that in time, carved wooden fish fillets, embedded in the same fancy sauce, were substituted for the real thing. The guests were none the wiser, but it was a sad day for the servants.)

All through this tale we see people playing mind games (except the servants), and not daring to be real. One-by-one, these

Chapter III – Knowledge for the Soul

'unworthies' passed the platter, secretly believing self to be worthy, in fact probably the only worthy one, but understanding that to say so would not be 'politically correct,' as the modern idiom puts it. Self-absorption is the poison; self-forgetfulness the antidote.

In the topsy-turvy Kingdom, those who exalt themselves will be humbled; those who humble themselves will be exalted. Sounds easy, doesn't it?

Please discuss the content of the article before considering the Reflection questions, Page 133.

Paul Stimson

Blessed Be the Sin

It is easier to make a saint out of a libertine than out of a prig.
(George Santayana, 1863-1952)

A nature program years ago gave a close-up look at the birth and rearing of bear cubs. At any sign of danger the mother signals cubs to climb the nearest tree and to remain until all is clear. In this as in all disciplinary matters, a noncompliance is sharply punished. When the mother eventually decides that it is time for them to be on their own she orders them up a tree, then walks away, never to be seen again. The cubs will remain aloft for an agonizingly long time, but eventually will have to face the great never-never and come down. So we see that their very first adult decision is one of defiance, overturning the sternest imperative they have ever been taught.

In most contemporary human cultures, whether religiously oriented or not, the first imperative to the young is "Be good." Motivation usually counts for naught; behavior is all that matters. It happens that there are more ill motivations for good behavior than good motivations, and mental-health professionals, decades later,

Chapter III – Knowledge for the Soul

are often asked to unscramble the wiring. It can be a formidable task.

'Most every grade-school student has heard the story of George Washington and the cherry tree: "Father, I cannot tell a lie. I cut it down with my hatchet." Why do we recall it so vividly, decades later? Could it be that such forthrightness is so uncommon as to stand almost alone in our experience? Many historians doubt that it happened, but it lives on because it links integrity to greatness.

We waffle, we weasel, we squirm. We learn early that if we can shift the blame, or belittle the wrongdoing, or come up with a justification, the punishment is reduced or eliminated. It all goes back to Adam, that clueless, gutless wonder who ate forbidden fruit, then passed the blame to " . . . *this woman that thou gavest me . . .* " That is what led theologians to their concept of Original Sin.

But in a closer look, we see two sins, not one —the violation of God's order, and the passing of the buck. It is always risky to compare the severity of sins, but the first one was absolutely bound to "happen." ("Happen" is in quotes because I am not a biblical literalist.) But let us rewind the tape and suppose that Adam might have mustered some humility and intestinal fortitude, as Washington did. "Yes, Lord, I ate it. I am truly sorry." We hope that God then, and Adam too, would have known that the relationship was restored. Consider, now, the intriguing possibility that the banishment from the Garden would not have been necessary. (But then, there would have been no story! Banishment from the Garden is the sole path to spiritual maturity.)

Thus, we can come to an understanding of Martin Luther's startling instruction, to sin boldly[39]. People who are preoccupied with avoidance of sin surely think Luther spoke heresy; let us revisit motivation, to clarify. Sin is sin only in that it is a violation of love. Love, therefore, is the only valid motive for avoiding sin. Jesus was fully tempted as we are, but did not sin, because—and only because—the desire to remain in loving relationship with God the Father was stronger than the urge to eat forbidden fruit. It will never be possible for us to bat a thousand as Jesus did, because we will not attain perfect love. But there is a paradox: relationships generally start smoothly, but invariably face one crisis after another. Each restoration adds strength, not merely getting back to where things would have been without the rupture, but tested, tried and true, and stronger than ever. Thus we echo through the ages, "Blessed be the sin."

Please discuss the content of the article before considering the Reflection questions, Page 133.

What Would the Disciples Do?

> *"...but stay in the city until you are clothed with power from on high."*
> *(Luke 24:49b)*

'What would Jesus do?' is so frequently asked that it has earned its own shorthand,'WWJD.' The attempted answers tend to be shallow and wide of the mark. A more apt question is suggested: 'What would the Disciples do?'

These uneducated fishermen, tax collectors, etc. are surely more understandable to our human frame. They sensed the Divinity of Jesus and followed faithfully, but time and again they misunderstood, jockeying for most-favored position. When defeat seemed near they all fled. After the Crucifixion, Peter announced that he was going fishing.

That should have been the end of it, if only human resources were in view. But they had been instructed to lay low and await the infilling of the Holy Spirit, and on that pivot point the history of civilization changed course, as never seen before or since. Suddenly that rag-tag band was single-minded, cohesive, fearless. Their foibles and frailties drifted to the background.

The Book of Acts of the Apostles recounts their fanning out into the world, changing minds and winning hearts. The pattern was the same everywhere; many people responded eagerly, but their secular leaders felt threatened. Converts, therefore, joined the Disciples in laying their lives on the line. Their core values thus came to light: anything worth living for is worth dying for. The Way, as it was first called, was at that stage unstoppable.

The leaders of the fledgling Church knew that the conversion experience was only a beginning. They established a pattern of training, typically of three years' duration, called the Catechumenate. The neophytes were admitted to the first part, the instructional part, of the worship service, but excluded from the Eucharist, the central act. At the Easter Vigil, after intense prayer and fasting, they were admitted. All this under threat of death at the hand of the Emperor..

In the Fourth Century AD, the Christian movement was suddenly legalized after the conversion of the Emperor Constantine, who sensed the inherent power of the movement and sought to harness that power to his own ends. This opportunism was a lasting stain on his conversion. The release from oppression was welcomed, but it had ironic consequences: suddenly, Christianity was not only legal but fashionable. The flood of 'converts' overwhelmed the Catechumenate. The tight discipline of the early Church was lost, but was replaced by a teaching ministry for the masses. The Spirit was now at work in a setting much more resembling the modern Church..

Chapter III – Knowledge for the Soul

The loss of the tight discipline and commitment has carried over. My father was not opposed to Sunday School, but once commented that childhood education in the Faith is for some a bit like a vaccination, which induces a mild form of the disease and a lasting immunity to the real thing. Human nature being as it is, the decline of fervor probably was inevitable. And it started very early indeed: in the letters to seven Churches, the Church at Laodicea is urged to be "*. . . hot or cold. If you are lukewarm I will spew you out of my mouth." (Revelation 3:15-16)*

Lukewarm, you see, has little effect on one's own life, and surely no impact on the life of another. Will we decide, hot or cold? Lukewarm is the default condition, and the choice of many church members today. Further, a Church that is an institution within the everyday world, is tempted as Jesus was at the beginning of his ministry. The tempter says, *"All these things (e.g., earthly power) will I give you if you will fall down and worship me (Luke 4:5-7)."*

And what would the Disciples do, if time-warped into our century? First, they would be astonished to find us still here. They truly believed that the Close of the Age was at hand. Yet they laid our groundwork, writing all their memorized words for our benefit, not their own. So, wouldn't they fit right in, shoulder-to shoulder with us? Perhaps indistinguishable from us?

Please discuss the content of the article before considering the Reflection questions, Page 134.

Paul Stimson

Scarcity & Abundance

> *I came that they may have life,*
> *and have it abundantly*
> *(John 10:10).*

During my years in oceanography, I spent a lot of time in Bermuda, where much of the food supply is imported from Great Britain. My recollection—perhaps a bit exaggerated—is that a pound of oatmeal came tightly compressed in a can, not much bigger than a Campbell's Soup can. It was a mirth-making thing to scoop out a cupful, day after day, and see the can still full to the brim as the contents decompressed. We were not fooled, of course: the can was soon empty. But in later years the flashback to that ever-full can has come to me frequently.

Children learn early that life is what has come to be called a zero-sum game. That means, in simplest terms, that if I give you a quarter of my candy bar, I will have only three quarters. Most parents are quick to lecture on the virtues of sharing, but real, live role models are seen less frequently.

The Scriptures are rife with reflections on this, the mind-set of scarcity: Now therefore thus says the Lord of hosts: *"Consider how you have fared. You have sown much and harvested little; you eat*

Chapter III – Knowledge for the Soul

but you never have enough; you drink but you never have your fill; you clothe yourselves but no one is warm; and he who earns wages earns wages to put them into a bag with holes . . . You have looked for much and lo, it came to little; and when you brought it home I blew it away. Why?" says the Lord of hosts. *"Because of my house that lies in ruins, while you busy yourselves each with his own house. Therefore the heavens above you have withheld the dew, and the earth has withheld its produce"* (Haggai 1:5-6, 9-10. See also Hosea 4:10, Micah 6:13-16, Isaiah 9:20).

Our earth-bound reaction to the threat of scarcity is to hoard all the more—to pull down our barns and build bigger (Luke 12:15-21). Laboratory rats that have once been subject to scarcity hoard from then on. The Mormons have a rule, full of earth-bound prudence, that every family store a two-year food supply—which is ineffective against three-year famines.

Also, I recall reading about a servant girl living in harsh conditions in Nineteenth-Century England. Her miserly master rationed everything; she was seen to be spooning the maximum allowance of sugar into her tea but not stirring it. "Well, I don't like it so sweet," she explained, "But I want my share."

Against this bleak backdrop, consider the promises of God and the mind-set of abundance. The prophet Joel first paints a desolate picture, then, urging his hearers to . . . *rend your hearts and not your garments* (2:13), he reverses the nay-sayers, promising: You shall eat in plenty and be satisfied, and praise the name of the Lord your God, who has dealt wondrously with you (2:26). In Luke we read: ...give and it will be given to you; good measure, pressed down, shaken together, running over, will be put into your lap (6:38). The vision is reinforced in countless other places, including . . . *My cup runneth over (Psalm 23:5)* and the Lilies of the field passage (Matthew 6:25-34), which goes on to urge . . . *do not be anxious about tomorrow.*

What do you hear me saying? Am I advocating imprudence and recklessness? Am I saying that generosity is a magic barrier against suffering? Certainly not. I am saying, among other things, that three-quarters (or, better still, one-half) of a candy bar eaten in community can be more gratifying than the whole bar eaten in isolation. I am saying, among other things, that this mind-set of scarcity or abundance affects the way we make decisions, at a level far deeper than common sense and conventional wisdom. In support of this, I note that someone once toured the skid-row section of a major city, talking with a large number of homeless men. Among them he found many who had once been prosperous; of these, he found not one who had been intentional about stewardship while he had the means to do so.

C. S. Lewis observed that when first things are placed first, second things are not diminished but enhanced[40].

Please discuss the content of the article before considering the Reflection questions, Page 134.

Chapter III – Knowledge for the Soul

Sin & Sanctity

> *All sins are attempts to fill voids.*[41]
> *(Simone Weil)*

Y'see, there's this humongous chalkboard in the sky, and whole regiments of angels keeping tallies of all the world's sins. Most sins are graded at one, two or three points each; the exception is sexual sin, where the minimum is 100 points. At night when most of us are asleep the angels use the free time to compute your DASQ (Daily Average Sin Quotient). There is a passing score but they won't tell you what it is. And, of course, they don't issue report cards. But if your DASQ rises to a point where even total reform and incorruptible purity of heart would not bring you down to a passing score in the remainder of your life span (which they know and you don't), they quietly stop counting: I mean, why waste chalk?

No? Have I got it all wrong?

I say to you, there is no motivation (other than fear, the worst of all motives) for avoidance of sinning that can be trusted to work for very long. If I should give up chocolate for Lent, and fail to come up with a better theology of self-denial than I had in school days (when I did give up chocolate for Lent), one of two things would happen: I would adopt one of a dozen unassailable rationalizations for—er—making today an exception, or if I succeeded, my soul would be further eroded by pride. Doing right things for wrong reasons earns few points on the Great Celestial Scoreboard.

We persist in looking at sins instead of the grand subject: sin. Sins are dealt with on the scale of minutes and seconds; sin is the big picture on a scale of years and decades. Sins can be committed or refused as spot decisions and for a range of motives (and fear is the flimsiest of these); sin can be met only by examining the spiritual warfare within. It is a process called sanctification.

I am indebted to my father for his vivid image of sin and sanctity. Picture yourself at the water's edge on a sunny day, as someone playfully splashes water at you. Your hot, dry skin feels the sting of every drop of cold water. Later, when you have been in the water and are thoroughly wet, the same splash is more vaguely felt and the individual drops no longer sting. We can learn to live in relative comfort in this wet condition, and we can depend on the process of living in this world to keep plenty of spray in the air. We can in time forget what it feels like to be warm and dry.

In this analogy, the first step toward sanctification is simply toweling off, then letting the warmth of the sun drive the moisture out of our pores. Restored to dryness, we feel once again the sting of each drop, and feel an urge to blot it dry. Warm, fluffy towels are yours for the asking. For details, see any priest.

Please discuss the content of the article before considering the Reflection questions, Page 135.

Chapter III – Knowledge for the Soul

Mystery

> *Let all mortal flesh keep silence,*
> *and with fear and trembling stand.*
> *(Liturgy of St. James)*[42]

Advent is a Mystery: it is a season of looking forward to a present Reality—the coming of the Christ. Christians must learn to live in this paradoxical sense of already-but-not-yet.

The things most of us have been taught about the laws of nature do not equip us well for this undertaking. It has been said that it takes 50 to 100 years for the learnings of science to sift down from scholarly journals into public awareness. Carl Sagan has tried to close that gap; in some sense he has done it well, but Sagan does not speak the Language of the Kingdom, so his teaching does little to inform our Christian perceptions.

Morton Kelsey[43] has written extensively about our "imprisonment" in the Space-Time Box —the popular notion that Reality is bounded by the three dimensions of space and one of time which our senses can perceive. We are inclined to disbelieve anything that seems not to fit the box, because we cannot imagine or understand it. And yet we do know better: we have only to look back a few centuries when few people had any grasp of why the sun rose each morning. Since celestial mechanics had not yet been conceived it was mostly seen as a paranormal event. Some cultures lived in dread that someday it would fail to rise; thus they centered their religion on a sun-god. As we learn more, the dividing line between the natural and the supernatural keeps moving. Within this earthly life, it will never disappear.

A century ago, a British clergyman named E. A. Abbott had a brilliant idea: people were already speculating about the existence of a fourth dimension, and the impossibility of sensing it. We can point forward and back, side-to-side and up-down, but all known directions are some combination of these three. Abbott conjectured a paper-thin, two-dimensional world whose inhabitants could point to a full circle around them, but could not conceive of up-down, much less point that way. "Flatland" is, in some ways, a silly book, but it gets across very well the idea of our inability to deal with spatial dimensions beyond the three we know so well. A Flatlander can go into a closet and close the door, believing that he is hidden from all, while we of the third dimension see all. The Flatlander's "skin" is a perimeter, an irregular line which surrounds all his innards. They are to his perception fully enclosed, but are exposed to our three-dimensional view. We can reach down and pluck out his gallstones with tweezers, without penetrating that skin, and he is hard pressed to believe that he is healed.

Fully 20% of the verses in the four Gospels are devoted to healings, all of them inexplicable. They are, if anything, harder for us to grasp than they were for the contemporaries of Jesus because we think we know everything. It is to me inconceivable that so much of his ministry would have been devoted to healing if it were not an integral element of Reality. I simply do not believe that God would have created the Universe, with its unfathomably intricate Laws, only to reserve the right to violate those Laws at his Almighty whim.

Some theologians, notably Barth and Bultmann, have tried to dismiss these inexplicable things, maintaining that the Scriptures contain quite enough that we can understand, and that we can found an adequate faith and practice on these. By Morton Kelsey's count, 46% of the verses in the New Testament deal with events and concepts that do not fit the Space-Time Box. If I could not integrate these into my faith, I would have no use for the other 54%.

Thus we kneel before the Altar, praying that we may be ... made one body with him, that he may dwell in us and we in him.

Experience trumps knowledge: do we need to understand?

Please discuss the content of the article before considering the Reflection questions, Page 135.

Warts and All

> *Be perfect, therefore,*
> *as your heavenly Father is perfect.*
> *(Matthew 5:48)*

C'mon, now: how are you going to connect that title to that scriptural text? I'll give you a hint: it all hinges on the definition of perfect—or rather of the Greek words which have been so translated. I can find seven such words which appear in the New Testament, and which look to my eye distinctly different one from another.

Only one of these, *akribeia*, denotes exactness. None of the others contains any hint of flawlessness, which is the sense brought to the above verse by most of us, most of the time. The word in Matthew is *teleios*, which carries meanings such as complete (in various applications of labor, growth, mental and moral character, etc.), and of full age. The related verb means set out for a definite point or goal; the root word describes the point aimed at. (For this, contrast the Greek word *hamartia* which is translated sin and literally means missing the mark, and so not sharing in the prize.)

God knows—far better than we ourselves do—that we are not flawless. Psalm 103 reassures us:

Chapter III – Knowledge for the Soul

As a father pities his children, so the LORD pities those who fear him.

For he knows our frame; he remembers that we are dust.

So the problem is not rooted in our flaws. Rather, we stumble in our misguided efforts to be flawless. Since we can never get there, we cap the frustration by diverting our energies to trying to appear flawless—perfect, that is, by our persistent mis-definition. That masking of our true selves (as Adam and Eve tried to hide in Eden) is at the root of our separation from God and our isolation from one another. The mask is difficult to sustain overtime, and despair threatens.

Many of us have had long experience of tangled relationships, and have come away with a deep, perhaps unconscious, learning that letting real feelings show is a risky undertaking. It exposes our warts. We cannot predict how others will react, especially if they, too, have trouble dealing with feelings. Instead of treasuring the knowing of each other, the game becomes one of manipulation, trying to control the feelings and interpretations of another. In the world of business and politics it is called public relations, and its practitioners have earned the derisive label, spin doctors. It doesn't work there, either.

Let's get real, folks (and I'm talking to myself, too): perfect, as used here, simply means perfectly human, perfectly fallible, hence perfectly lovable. Think about that: a person with all flaws plainly visible is, in the eyes of God, perfectly lovable. The great barrier to love is not our flaws, but our attempt—always unsuccessful—to hide those flaws.

The school of my youth had a Latin motto which I didn't grasp until decades later: *Esse quam videri*. It means, simply, be what you appear to be. No, not reveal what you are, but be what you appear to be. In other words, if you are going to put up a front, you'd better start growing into it. It is the path toward completeness, toward maturing, toward becoming of full age, toward perfection—warts and all.

Please discuss the content of the article before considering the Reflection questions, Page 135.

Chapter III – Knowledge for the Soul

Earth & Heaven

> *It is since Christians have largely ceased to think of the other world that they have become so ineffective in this. Aim at Heaven and you will get earth thrown in; aim at earth and you will get neither[44].*
>
> *(C. S. Lewis)*

Decades ago I heard a withering quip about a Churchman: "He is so Heavenly-minded, he is no earthly good." At the opposite pole, how many of us experience any stirring of mind, heart and spirit when Heaven is mentioned?

Let us ponder: somewhere in your past is a time and place which floods you with nostalgia whenever you think of it. Close your eyes and you can almost get into the there-and-then of it. We cannot do the same with Heaven, of course, because it is not in our index of memories. And, let's face it: the images we have been given—Pearly Gates, Golden Street, harp-wielding angels—don't cut very deep.

We are imprisoned in time and space—the work of Creation. Heaven lies beyond these. I think of it as a state of being, without really knowing what that might mean. But the promises—face-to-face communion with God and with all who have gone before us, the eradication of sin, the unveiling of Mystery—are fodder for a life-time of imagining, if only we open ourselves to them.

Those of you who recognize these words: . . . the communion of saints, the forgiveness of sins, the resurrection of the body, and the life everlasting. Amen—try immersing yourself in them, instead of parroting.

Please discuss the content of the article before considering the Reflection questions, Page 136.

Chapter III – Knowledge for the Soul

One Flesh

> *Therefore a man leaves his father and his mother and cleaves to his wife, and they become one flesh.*
> *(Genesis 2:24)*
> *They are therefore no longer two, but one flesh.*
> *(Matthew 19:6)*

One flesh? You mean, like, I can gain weight from what my spouse eats? Hardly. The Eastern use of vivid overstatement gets its point across, but only a few tragic fools have taken such hyperbole literally. At issue here is the concept of marriage as radically different from all other forms of human relationship, and pointing to a depth of connectedness like no other.

"Good fences make good neighbors" is a widely accepted notion of the way the world works. Most of us have good relations with neighbors most of the time, but always under a watchful eye: my neighbor's self-interests may well be in conflict with mine. The fence might be a physical barrier or a figurative line in the sand, but its intent is mutually understood.

Most married couples naturally and easily draw closer than this. Single-mindedly, they fight off any external threat. The need to share and share alike is generally well understood, but ambivalence lurks beneath the surface. What to do if the cake got cut to an odd number of slices? How far can I press my wants without being labeled a nag or a slacker?

But in a living individual, e.g., 'one flesh', these interior stresses are absent. It would be quite abnormal for one hand to attempt to weaken the other, for the purpose of maintaining the upper hand. It would be utterly illogical for the left brain to ridicule the creativity of the right. The abdominal muscles could strangulate the intestines if they so choose, but they do know better. All these components of the body know that their identity as organs is subordinate to the body, and their interdependence is total. A cancerous cell, living in defiance of this principle, ultimately seeks to destroy itself along with the body it kills.

Throughout nature we see a paradoxical principle: one must be willing to lose in order to gain. A seed contains an ability to become a plant, but first must submit to burial in wet earth. You could not convince a caterpillar that those were its parents who just flew by; in order to grow those gossamer wings, it must undergo a transformation that must feel like dying. The forging of a couple from two individual people is a transformation of similar scope. The sole pathway to this state is best expressed as mutual surrender. Will we agree to die to self, so the couple may live?

Sadly, the answer for most couples seems to be "No." Marriage is a union in the spiritual realm, and its demands will forever be in conflict with the urges of the flesh. Get used to it; we will never cease stumbling. But the spiritual side of this tug-of-war is relentless, and most of us will help each other up, dusting off and bandaging wounds, till death do us part. We do not cease to live our lives as individuals, of course, but as the distinction between individual wants and the needs of the couple comes into a sharper focus, we will tend ever more toward the higher good. Gradually, painfully we learn that we cannot do it alone: Higher Power, God, Yahweh, Allah, by whatever Name known is forever the Source of the vision and the Way to its fulfillment.

May the Force be with you.

Please discuss the content of the article before considering the Reflection questions, Page 136.

Come, Labor On.[45]

> *"...Who dares stand idle on the harvest plain, While all around us waves the golden grain?"*
> *(Jane Laurie Borthwick).*

I still associate this hymn with the end of summer and the dreaded start of school. In the course of twelve years of Episcopal schooling (and compulsory daily worship) I memorized hundreds of hymns, without effort or intention. It bothered me, though, that I could mouth the words without connecting one line with the next, and sometimes I looked back to see what I had sung.

The Hymnal has been called the layman's book of theology. Come, Labor On picks up on the Gospel-borne metaphor of the harvest to illuminate our hope of Salvation and our mission of evangelism. The hymn was written in the 19th Century, when we were far more a nation of farmers than now; central heating and indoor plumbing were rarities and air conditioning nonexistent. How heedful of God to give us temperate weather at the seasons of heaviest effort—planting and harvesting—and to give us an excuse for holing up when it is too hot or too cold. We have lost something

Chapter III – Knowledge for the Soul

vital in our modern economy, which urges, even compels, that we run full-throttle for 48 or 50 weeks of the year.

Idle time need not be lost time: new learnings need time to interweave with the old. Spiritual formation and communion with God demand time set apart. To get it, we must buck the tide of culture and set time apart. Without it, our busyness is vanity—which, in Hebrew, means emptiness.

Please discuss the content of the article before considering the Reflection questions, Page 137.

Reflection Questions, Chapter III

Evil

1) What is your concept of Satan? Has it changed as you have matured?
2) Do you think there are different forms of evil? Why or why not?
3) When do you find it easiest to be Christ-like? When is it hardest?
4) List examples of evil in our world today. What tools of resistance are available to you?
5) List examples of good in our world today. What habits encourage goodness?
6) Where are you most vulnerable to evil?
7) How have you been successful in overcoming evil in the past?

The Power of Satan

1) What is your personal understanding of the devil?
2) What is the track record on your "discernment meter"? How well can you tell what is of God, of Man, of Satan?
3) How do you go about letting God into your life? What ways of opening yourself up have you found to be helpful?

4) How hard is it to let go of the hope that Satan will keep his promises and reach for God?
5) Share your personal experiences/successes.

The Will of God

1) 1.What must we do to receive the Power of God?
2) 2.What keeps you from adjusting the pattern of your life to become part of God's?
3) 3. Think of a time when you notably heeded the instructions of the Patriarch, and wove just right. Are you aware that you were a co-operator in fulfilling the Mind of the Maker?
4) 4. Think of a time when you didn't. Are you aware that you permanently altered the outcome? Was the rug still beautiful?

Judgment Day

1) Do you have a personal concept of afterlife? Why or why not?
2) Do you have a personal concept of judgment? Why or why not?
3) What experiences would you like to have as part of your own afterlife?

Was Jesus Christ Sinless?

1) What temptations do you find it hardest to resist?
2) What motives cause you to sin most often: pride? fear? apathy? selfishness? ignorance?
3) Can love cause you to sin?

4) What tools for resisting temptation work best for you?

Incarnation

1) What adjectives best describe God for you?
2) What activities of adoration will you take on this Advent?
3) Advent: He came as a child at Bethlehem, He comes into our hearts at Christmas, and he will come at the end of time. Like a good Boy Scout, be prepared!

Faith

1) How uncomfortable are you with doubt and uncertainty in your daily life?
2) How can you take the first baby steps of faith in the Christian God if you have been raised by an abusive father?
3) How would you try to convey the Power and the Love of God to a pagan?

Predestination

1) What is your understanding of the definition of spiritual Predestination?
2) Do you think it is possible to predict the outcome of some people's destinies?
3) Can individuals change their destinies? If not, Why? If so, What does it take to do so?

4) How comfortable are you with the concept of an "eternal now", knowing that a loving God is with you?
5) How have you personally experienced God's plan for you?
6) What would "being ready" for the end time look like for you?

Vulnerability

1) Of what is your shell made?
2) How can you become more actively vulnerable for God?
3) Comment: I love. Therefore I am vulnerable.
4) Comment: I do not love. Therefore I am safe.

Worthiness

1) What gifts has God given you that are worthy of bragging?
2) When does humility get in the way of honesty?
3) When bragging, to whom do you compare yourself?
4) When being humble, to whom do you compare yourself?

Blessed Be the Sin

1) When has an understanding of sin brought you closer to God?
2) Is any category of sin 'better' or worse than another (sins of ignorance, omission, commission, etc.)?
3) .What, in fact, defines a really, really bad sin? Getting caught? The harm to others? The consequences to me?

4) Sin separates us from God. How can anything good come out of sin?

What Would the Disciples Do?

1) Are you hot, cold, or lukewarm? How is your Church?
2) Name some "saints" who have impressed you by their ministry of caring.
3) Can you name any Christian "world-changers" who are at work today?
4) The three temptations by Satan in Luke 4:1-13 might be "Feed them and they'll believe," "Bow down to me and receive earthly power", and "Wow them with miracles and they will believe." How has the church succeeded or failed in these temptations? Through history? Recently?

Scarcity & Abundance

1) How would you define earthly abundance?
2) How would you define spiritual abundance?
3) What earthly things, when shared, enhance abundance for all?
4) What things in your own life do you need to give away?
5) Share your personal experiences with earthly and spiritual scarcity..... with abundance.
6) What keeps you from trusting God for your abundance?

Sin & Sanctity

1) If you were offered a glimpse of the Great Chalkboard, would you like to see it?
2) How "wet" with sin are you? 10%? 20%? 50%?
3) How is your towel supply?
4) Do you like the way your life is going? Do you want to change direction?
5) If "feeling the sting of each drop" of our sins is the beginning of sanctification, to what should this lead? Where does it end?
6) Criticize: "I'm going to get myself sanctified even if it kills me!"

Mystery

1) How comfortable are you with "Holy Mysteries?"
2) Do you need to understand?
3) Discuss: not all things without explanation are miracles, but all miracles lack space-time explanation because the cause is outside space-time

Warts and All

1) Make a list of your 'warts.' Which of them might you open to the transforming power of God?

2) Which of them must you learn to love, and ask others to love?
3) Mull over: For God's sake (and your own), forget about trying to earn love. Accept it and respond. Build the other person up in truth and you are fulfilling the law.

Earth & Heaven

1) Do you imagine death as the end of life, or as a change of state?
2) When you think of Judgment Day, are you afraid?
3) What do you think of the idea that Hell is only for people who would not like Heaven?
4) When your naked soul is clothed in a resurrection body fit for eternity, what relationships will you seek?

One Flesh

1) What have you been willing to give up to strengthen a relationship?
2) What does it mean spiritually when two become one?
3) What are the possibilities when one partner desires to form 'One Flesh' and the other doesn't?
4) How does a relationship grow from sexual attraction that demands, to a shared love that builds each other up?
5) Do you know couples that have become 'one flesh?' What are they like?
6) In what ways does your marriage differ from close friendship?

Chapter III – Knowledge for the Soul

7) How do external pressures help or interfere?
8) What cancerous cells have survived in the One Flesh which is your marriage?

Come, Labor On

1) When do you make time in your schedule to sit quietly with God?
2) What hymn texts have special meaning for you?
3) How can you avoid letting your job consume you?

Chapter IV –
Knowledge for the Mind

"To know you is to love you" is a recurring theme in popular music. Knowing about you is one element of this, and knowing you, in a deeper, less tangible sense, is quite another.

"Know" is a broad spectrum word through the ages. In both the Old and the New Testament it denotes sexual intercourse.

Our primary source for knowing God is, of course, the Bible. Knowing about is mainly in the prose; knowing in the poetry.

Paul Stimson

Symbols of the Holy Trinity

> *Then God said: "Let us make man in our image, after our likeness..."*
> *(Genesis 1:26)*

A small town, once upon a time, had only one barber. That barber shaved all the men in town, except those who shaved themselves. The question arose: who shaves the barber? Every attempt to answer with a simple, declarative statement can be countered with another, seemingly logical, and some might think it could be resolved only by the barber growing a beard. Thus a simple, logical fallacy masquerades as a genuine paradox, which it most certainly is not.

For contrast, ponder the elegantly simple, simply elegant, Möbius Strip. If you are not already familiar with this concept  please take a moment to make one; it will help greatly to convey the concept. Start by cutting a strip of paper, ½ inch wide by about 6 inches long, and taping the ends together into a ring. Clearly it has an inside surface and an outside surface, and there is no mistaking

Chapter IV – Knowledge for the Mind

one for the other. You can even turn it inside out, but still the surfaces are distinct.

But now pull it apart at the tape and give one end of the strip a half twist, before sticking it back together. You have made a Möbius Strip, a genuine, irresolvable, paradox. As you pick it up you can make the clear, undeniable statement that your thumb is on one side of the strip and your forefinger on the other, and that will be forever true no matter where you pick it up. But set about to color one side of it with a crayon, and you will go twice around, returning to your starting point. Irrefutably, the strip has only one surface, which you have just colored. There is no logical trap to be sprung; the paradox is here to stay.

One day, decades ago, I was pondering the theological concept of the Holy Trinity, which posits One God in Three Persons. There is no direct mention of Trinity in the Bible, 'though there are many hints of it. "I and the Father are One," said Jesus (John 10:30); the Letter of Jude says (v.20):" But you, Beloved, build yourselves up in your most holy faith; pray in the Holy Spirit; keep yourselves in the love of God; wait for the mercy of our Lord Jesus Christ unto eternal life." The concept of Triune God developed experientially in people living the Faith.

I thought about the several attempts to illustrate the idea, beginning with St. Patrick and his three-leaf clover, through the fleur-de-lis, and on to the three interlocking Borromean Rings (which many of us recognize as the Ballantine logo.) All these fail to convey any hint of the Mystery

at the heart of the concept: each of them comprises three distinct objects, however interconnected.

As I contemplated, a Möbius strip coalesced in my mind's eye, with its ribbon-like cross-section now expanded into a triangle. Thus, the Trinity Ring came into being. At any point on the circumference you can place three fingers on three surfaces, but tracing it with a finger, three times around, you discover that the three faces are one.

There is no point at which one ends and another begins.

Does the Trinity Ring have three faces? Yes. Does it have only one surface? Yes. The veracity of two statements that in common logic ought to be mutually exclusive, is the hallmark of genuine paradox.

But wherein is this important enough to write about? Advocates of the other monotheistic religions tend to scoff at Christianity's claim of belonging to the club. Yes, the concept of Triune God is complex, but who is to say it has to be simple in order to be true? It

Chapter IV – Knowledge for the Mind

is not an intellectual construct; the human trinity of heart, soul and mind must converge on it.

Athanasius (c.297-373), an early Bishop of Alexandria, thought it important enough to merit a lengthy and deliberately redundant creed. He presses the point "...*For there is one Person of the Father, another of the Son, and another of the Holy Ghost...But the Godhead of the Father, of the Son, of the Holy Ghost, is all one, the Glory equal, the Majesty co-eternal...The Father eternal, the Son eternal, and the Holy Ghost Eternal. And yet there are not three eternals, but one eternal...*" (Book of Common Prayer 1979, pp 864-5).

Point well taken.

Please discuss the content of the article before considering the Reflection questions, Page 173.

Paul Stimson

Our Worm's-Eye View of Reality

A Response to all who reject the concept of Holy Trinity

Science has made astounding progress in the past 100 years. We now can see very nearly to the most distant objects in our expanding universe. Since a view of vast distance is equivalent to a look back in time, we are seeing nearly back to the creation event, informally known as the 'Big Bang.' There is no expectation that we will ever see the moment of creation, let alone the Creator who lies behind it.

All our knowledge of this universe is rooted in an assumption that the laws of physics operate uniformly throughout it. But all three monotheistic religions agree that God (or *Allah* or *Yahweh*) lies outside God's creation, where we have no basis for any assumptions.. We are agreed that Eternal God is not traveling through time with us, and to think of Heaven as a place stretches the definition of 'place.' The wispy fragments we 'know' have come to us from God, through revelation.

We mortals, from the moment of birth, build much of our knowledge base by relating new information to what we already know. Among the tools for this are analogy, simile and metaphor,

Chapter IV – Knowledge for the Mind

but the understanding they convey is incomplete in varying degrees and is subject to misunderstanding. We say this new thing is like that already-known thing, and it usually gets across. But how would you describe a vivid sunset to a person born color-blind, for whom all creation is reduced to shades of gray? The emotion in your words will come through, but blazing scarlets and subtle amethysts are meaningless.

Thus, by analogy, we grasp God's problem in attempting to convey the nature of God and the Kingdom of Heaven to 'color-blind' mortals. Calling on my own Christian background, I note the number of times Jesus introduced an analogy with the words, "The Kingdom of Heaven is like ..." Note, though, that the similes were meant to be grasped at an emotional and spiritual level: in no case do they point to physical reality. Therefore, we must eschew literalism: those elements not analogous must be discarded.

The terms Father, Son and Holy Spirit convey something of the relationships within the Holy Trinity. To suggest that the Father would have to have intercourse with the Virgin Mary to beget the Son flies in the face of the very concept of analogy. It is like saying that if "My Love is like a red, red rose," it must have thorns. Someone has suggested a metaphor that reaches me deeply: the Father is the Lover, the Son is the Beloved, and the Holy Spirit is the Love that flows between them. That one is far more difficult to misapprehend.

A century ago, more or less, physics was asserting that the atom was the ultimate indivisible unit of matter, never dreaming that the study of sub-atomic particles would in time give way to the study of sub-sub-atomic particles. It is short-sighted to give an absolute status to our tentative theorems; it is perilous to label as false those truths that are yet beyond our reach. The Earth was once flat, and our Galaxy was, in the next immature declaration, deemed to be the entire Universe.

It is often said that we are merely sojourners on this planet—that our ultimate home is in the world to come. St. Paul clearly understood this when he spoke of our seeing "through a glass darkly" those things that will be understood later. Perhaps, in the perspective of Eternity, we are like babies in the womb, who can sense mother's emotions, can hear sounds from the world outside, but otherwise have only wispy hints of the life that lies ahead.

Please discuss the content of the article before considering the Reflection questions, Page 173.

Chapter IV – Knowledge for the Mind

Time & Eternity

When We've been there ten thousand years, Bright shining as the sun, We've no less days to sing God's praise Than when we'd first begun. –
John Rees[46]

The Roman god Janus had faces on both the front and the back of his head. The month of January, a time for looking back on the old year and ahead to the new, is named for him.

We speak of past, present and future as if we understood what we are talking about. Past and future, in fact, seem to have simple, comprehensible meaning, but present is the slippery one: we can use it to mean this century, my lifetime, or today, narrowing down to a steadily moving instant which divides the past from the future. Think about it: when you are in the middle of saying "now," the "n" is already in the past and the "w" is still in the future—however fast you say it. The present, in this sense, has zero duration.

I have read Stephen Hawking's *Brief History of Time* with considerable care, but still have no gut feeling for what the physicists mean when they speak of the four (and more) dimensions of Space-Time. It seems that their mathematics treats space and time as almost interchangeable. One of the foundational concepts of modern physics is that there appears to be no such thing as absolute time. If you set up two perfect clocks side-by-side, they will keep identical time forever. But if you carry one across the room it will fall behind, and if you carry it back to the starting point it will fall behind still more. The discrepancy is far too small to measure, but it is real. Please don't ask me to explain further.

The Scriptures give us clues that the concepts of time and eternity are interwoven with the Mysteries of the Kingdom. Science-fiction writers are fond of time warps, but the Bible can outdo the best of them: ...with the Lord, one day is as a thousand years, and a thousand years as one day (2 Peter 3:8). This verse gives a glimpse of how it can be that God, who encompasses all history, has time to number the hairs of our heads and grieve over each sparrow as it falls (Luke 12:6 –7). We speculate that God sees space-time laid out as a continuum from beginning to end, whereas we see only the present, and remember the past. And the end, of course, changes as we make decisions.

We are assigned the task of learning to view time from this elusive perspective of eternity. The much-misunderstood, much-abused concept of predestination has been warped by our worm's-eye view; it has been taken to mean that it doesn't matter what we say or do, because our salvation/damnation has already been decided. Not so, dear friends: the fact that the outcome is known in Eternity takes nothing away from our calling to walk in Love as Christ loved us, to work out our salvation in fear and trembling.

It is often heard that survivors of near-death experience saw their whole life flash before their eyes. Raymond Moody[47] and Elizabeth Kubler-Ross[48] have confirmed this in their studies. I had long pictured it as something like the fast-forward button on a VCR; lately I have come to think of it more as a panorama, in which the physicists' four dimensions of space-time are somehow "seen" in a continuum of here and now.

Yahweh is one of the Hebrew names of God. It literally means I am. Jesus said ... *before Abraham was, I am (John 8:58)*. Eternity, I perceive, is not an infinitely long time: it is an unfolding of the instantaneous present into timeless, eternal now.

Please discuss the content of the article before considering the Reflection questions, Page 174.

Paul Stimson

The Spiritual Dimension

> *...the Kingdom of God is within you.*
> *(Luke 17:21)*

It is frustrating to ponder the fourth dimension of space: we cannot imagine a direction we might point that isn't just a combination of the familiar three dimensions. But we can learn something by considering a two-dimensional being, perhaps looking to us like a cartoon character, whose home is like an infinitesimally thin sheet of paper. North-south and east-west are familiar dimensions but up-down is meaningless and unimaginable.

Two-dimensional creatures can go into a room and close the door, thinking they are in complete privacy, but we of the third dimension can look down on them and see everything. 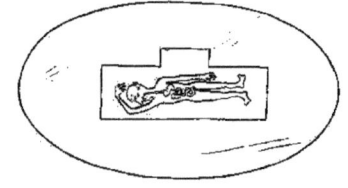 The unperceivable third dimension would be to them the spiritual dimension—source of unfathomable events that defy the laws of nature, to the best of their understanding of those laws. We

Chapter IV – Knowledge for the Mind

of the third dimension might look closely at his innards and spot a gallstone. Reaching in with tweezers we might pluck it out — without penetrating his skin!

Much has been written about the fourth dimension as our spiritual dimension, but the concept needs to be brought closer to the world of our experience. Stay with us through some simple illustrations, and your horizons will expand. First we must come to an understanding that the three-dimensional world so familiar to us is actually seen in two dimensions, because: the retina of the eye is effectively a two-dimensional surface, and our perception of the third dimension comes only through the brain's astonishing ability to process what we see. If we look at a cube made of transparent plastic the image on the retina is sketched in **Figure 1**. Through long experience we have learned to construe this two-dimensional image as a three-dimensional cube. We see it as two overlapping squares and four diagonal connecting lines of the third dimension. A draftsman might draw the two squares the same size but an artist, aware of the rules of perspective, would draw the farther square smaller than the nearer. The diminution of dimensions with distance is a vital part of our ability to interpret what we see.

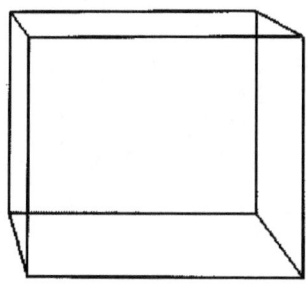

Figure 1

We might label the square's dimensions as height and width; to transform a two-dimensional square into a three-dimensional cube we must project it in a direction called depth. If the fourth dimension is real—and science is confident that it is—we should be able to project our cube in yet another direction and form a hypercube. Sounds easy enough, but when we ponder doing it we are stopped cold: in what direction do we move it?

Our two-dimensional creature could theorize a cube, and could see and interpret its shadow, which is **Figure 1**, on his world. In like manner our hypercube casts its shadow on three-dimensional space, but we have no direct way of seeing it: we might have to use holographic techniques. But here a delightful surprise: the three-dimensional shadow projects onward to a two-dimensional screen, and we can comprehend it! A cube within a cube, **Figure 2**, farther away in the

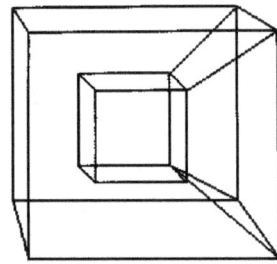

Figure 2

direction of the fourth dimension and therefore smaller. A label for this new direction springs instantly to mind—inward and outward—and these we recognize as the key words of all spiritual experience. (For clarity we have omitted four of the eight fourth-dimensional edges from Figure 2.) To keep our frame of reference clear, note that we familiarly use inward and outward in a purely three-dimensional sense—into and out of our house—but this usage is something else.

Chapter IV – Knowledge for the Mind

To envision how action in the fourth dimension might impact our world, let us revisit our two-dimensional friend. Suppose we built a cone and moved it up through his plane from below. He would first see a point appear out of nowhere; as the cone moved through his world he would see a steadily expanding circle which would just as abruptly vanish a short time later. The analog of this for a hypercone of the fourth dimension passing through our world would be the sudden appearance of a point in space, growing to an ever-larger sphere until abruptly vanishingly. I am glad God is not a practical joker, because he really could jerk us around!

Let us apply this concept to some old problem areas: all that stuff in the Bible that couldn't actually have happened, but we accept it because the Bible says so, and who dares to argue? Take Moses and the burning bush, which flamed away but wasn't consumed. God doesn't jerk us around, I'm confident, but to create a scene which will still have impact thousands of years later, what would be wrong with injecting a little celestial propane mixed with heavenly fire-retardant? Vastly more important, ponder the thirteen post-Resurrection appearances of Jesus, reported in the four Gospels, in which, if one looks closely, every one of them has aspects which seem to violate the laws of physics. Showing up in the Upper Room, with all the doors locked? Appearing out of nowhere on the road to Emmaus? Jesus, I am convinced, went out of his way to show that his resurrection body was a real body, by eating fish with them on the shore of Galilee, but somehow it was more than real—perhaps surreal.

The Bible verse quoted in the subtitle — Luke 17:21—is at the heart of our story. The Pharisees challenged Jesus, asking him (with tongue in cheek) when God's Kingdom was coming. Jesus' simple reply made it clear that it is not a matter of when—the Kingdom of God is within you here and now. The verse has been the source of much perplexity over the centuries, because most people's minds are locked into our three-dimensional Universe and think that is all there is to Reality. He came to tell us there is more to it. He couldn't describe it directly to our worm's-eye view, so used much metaphor and simile: the Kingdom is this and that; is like this, that and the other thing. And in that worm's-eye view we have trouble grasping how the Kingdom could be within, so some translators have fudged the wording, saying instead that the Kingdom is in the midst of us. Maybe that is easier to swallow, but the Greek word at issue is *entos*—which simply means within in this writer's lexicon.

Saint Paul noted that we see 'through a glass darkly.' But let us use our God-given skills to see all we are able to.

Please discuss the content of the article before considering the Reflection questions, Page 174.

Chapter IV – Knowledge for the Mind

Either/Or versus Both/And

> Behold, I make all things new.
> (Revelation 21:5)

Charles Darwin's second book was titled, "The Descent of Man." Many people are affronted by the idea of being descended from apes; somehow it is even more threatening than discovering a criminal or a politician in the lineage. But there is an old doggerel, written purportedly by an ape and recounting outrageous deeds of mankind, which no self-respecting ape would consider. The final couplet is unforgettable:

Yes, man descended, the ornery cuss —
But Brother, he didn't descend from us!

Could it be that many of the people who argue stridently over the tension between the writings of Darwin and the Book of Genesis have not given more than a cursory glance to either? Or, if they have studied Genesis, have they overlooked what is known about the origin and intent of the story? Genesis was among the last of the books of the Hebrew Scriptures — the Old Testament — to be written down. For uncounted centuries, the several myths compiled into the book were in the oral tradition, passed from generation to generation by word of mouth.

Myth is a word that has lost its meaning in modern usage. Most people think it is a catch-all label for things that are not true; in fact, it denotes deeper truths told by fictional means. Six-year-old fans of Dr. Seuss understand this. The ancient myth-makers, perhaps tribal leaders in the Land of Israel, pondered their plight as deeply flawed creatures of all-powerful, all-loving God, and imagined apples, serpents and fig-leaves as analogies, just as Dr. Seuss conjured up Star-bellied Sneetches to point up the absurdity of prejudice.

The popular criticism of Darwin centers on matters he never addressed. Creationism? Intelligent Design? Surely he would have pronounced them beyond the scope of scientific inquiry — and he was a scientist, through and through. Does that mean he would have ruled out the possibility of their place in reality? No, he was a trained thinker, and he would have known better.

Most of us, not-so-well-trained thinkers, do not handle complexities and subtleties so well. We pride ourselves on our rationality, but emotion can trump reason at every turn. When a widespread disagreement has gone unresolved for a long time it turns into polarization, and the opposing camps see each other as enemies. And enemies must be defeated, by fair means or foul. The foul means can include oversimplifying, distorting, trivializing and demonizing the opposing view.

The upshot is that when an either-or polarization is in the air, hardly anyone stops to consider the possibility of both-and. Which is predominant in our formation as people, genetics or environment? This nature vs. nurture disagreement has been in the air for

Chapter IV – Knowledge for the Mind

generations; the rational conclusion seems to be both-and, inseparably and interactively.

As we seek to comprehend nature, we find ever-increasing complexity in all directions. At the dawn of the 20th Century, Science sincerely believed that we knew almost everything. A notable physicist, addressing a graduating class, sympathized with them because the pioneering was all done, and there was so little more to investigate. Atoms were long thought to be the indivisible, fundamental particles; in time we learned that they are composed of protons, neutrons and electrons. Indivisible sub-atomic particles? No, the field of sub-sub-atomic particles keeps digging deeper, finding quarks, bosons and gluons. Will scientists of the 22nd Century be studying sub-sub-sub-sub-atomic particles?

And into the growing complexity, paradox enters. Einstein once remarked that reality is not only queerer than we suppose, it is queerer than we are able to suppose. Let us disabuse ourselves of any notion that we will find our way into the Mind of the Maker. But, rather than remain in the present morass, let us examine three terms that are central to the discussion: creation, intelligent design, and evolution, and see what can be dispassionately said about them.

Creation implies that our present reality had a beginning. This is not a long-standing assumption; some astronomers a century ago believed in a steady-state Universe that simply had always existed. Creationists today divide into two camps, one believing the age of the Universe to be about 13 billion years, and the other something less than 10,000 years, with nothing in between. In the United States today the split is something like 60/40, so neither side can rationally ignore the other. In neither purported event were there journalists on the scene, so both sides extract their inferences from what can be seen now.

Intelligent Design is an ages-old concept. The Psalmist wrote, *"The Heavens declare the Glory of God, and the Firmament telleth His Handiwork."* Physicists inform us that the Creator had to start by inventing the laws of physics: if the physical constants were altered so much as a hair's breadth, there would be no stars or planets. No telescope can grasp immensity; no microscope can resolve the intricacy of a single atom. The ninety-two natural elements are capable of interacting in a near-infinity of compounds; the vastness of energy is beyond imagination. Was it all created just for us, on this one minuscule planet? We surely do behave as if it has been.

Evolution is the inflammatory word. Young-Earth proponents are strident in labeling it 'only a theory,' but it is not seen just in the fossil record: real-time breeding records of domestic animals show the mechanism clearly at work. To those who refuse to read and heed we can offer only a polite farewell: no further dialog is possible. Those still on board might point out that evolutionary improvement of a species is one thing, but evolution of one species into another is conceptually different. But when a sub-species has isolated itself to the point where it no longer consents to interbreed with the parent species, by definition, a new species has arisen — a

Chapter IV – Knowledge for the Mind

new species that can be expected to continue diverging from its parent. Again, we must say farewell to dissenters.

Searching the above for all that is non-contradictory, what synthesis can we construct? All who subscribe to the concept of a created Universe must consider whether it could have created itself, and if not, there must have been a creator, generally named God, Allah or Yahweh, among other names. And if that creation shows signs of having been intelligently designed, there must have been an intelligent designer on the team. Again, we assign the name of God. We have thus covered the who, what and where; the remaining questions center on the when, why and how.

On the when question, the two sides differ by six orders of magnitude, and neither side will listen to the arguments of the other, so no resolution is foreseeable. Why is a fascinating question, but beyond the scope of objective inquiry. Surely the Creator is a Lover, intent upon creating objects for that love. Both sides might agree that the urge to create is a compelling force in any creative being, and the Creator will forever astonish us with the ingenuity, resourcefulness and interactiveness of the how. Either Creation or Evolution? Why is it difficult to grasp the both/and? Surely our Creator is clever enough — and wise enough — to create an evolving Universe.

Please discuss the content of the article before considering the Reflection questions, Page 174.

Paul Stimson

The Hebrew Scriptures

> *So Philip ran to him and heard him reading Isaiah the prophet, and asked, "Do you understand what you are reading?" And he said, "How can I, unless someone guides me?"*
> *(Acts 8:30b –31)*

Many of the adult Christians I have talked to are squeamish about the Old Testament— which is, these days, often referred to as The Hebrew Scriptures. They dislike all the destruction and bloodletting, and all the actions attributed to an angry, vengeful God. To this day there are many leaders, who call themselves Christians yet miss the Good News entirely, ruling by fear rather than winning through love, as if the wrath of God were not reaching all who deserve or "need" it.

One of my friends, Gerry, was subjected to an extraordinarily heavy dose of this mistreatment (which has aptly been labeled Spiritual Abuse). Growing up in wartime England, he was sent to a church-run boarding school at age six, where they tried to scare him into "being good," and repeatedly slammed his head against the wall when he wasn't. Through persistent questioning and challenging, he earned a heavier dose of abuse than did most of his classmates.

Chapter IV – Knowledge for the Mind

The Hebrew Scriptures are, quite simply, the writings of a people who perceived themselves called by God, and their struggle to understand and respond to that call. Theologians call it Salvation History. The writings contain much which is deeply embarrassing to the people of Israel, and which would have been cleaned up by a people of secular mind-set. Some of the writings are factual and historical but more are mythical. (Myth is a seriously misunderstood concept in this age: myth uses less-than-factual means to tell deeper-than-factual truth.)

The writers tried by every means to tell the good news, that God made us and loves us, and asks only that we respond to that love. The Law was given, if only to show us that law cannot save us. The prophets saw the anger of God—the anger of love disappointed—and saw God's ceaseless efforts to call us into relationship, with him and with each other. The prophets also foresaw that none could save us except a Savior—and foretold not a conquering hero but a suffering servant.

People see what they are conditioned to see. The church-trained people who abused Gerry had no vision of the Kingdom of Heaven and certainly could find all the justification they wanted for their actions, looking only at the evidence of anger and not the unflagging love that lay just behind it. Gerry hung on for many years, out of fear for what would happen if he didn't. Eventually he lost his desire to spend Eternity with this angry, punishing God.

To focus on the New Testament without a grasp of all that went before is to start reading the latter chapters of a book, seeing words and actions that make no sense. The Creation Story (wherein myth once again uses fiction to tell a deeper truth) gives us deep insight into the Nature and Love of God, insight which was until recently dismissed by science, but which now seems to anticipate and underlie our understanding of cosmology. *"Let there be light"* (Genesis 1:2) is the first step in creation: sounds like the "Big Bang" to me. The Abraham-Isaac story (Genesis 22) anticipates the Cross, and opens the paradox of love and obedience mingled, even in all-powerful God.

Gerry has had a conversion experience. His turning point was one sentence in the writings of J. R. R. Tolkein[49]: *"The story of Christ is simply a true myth: a myth working on us the same way as the others, but with this tremendous difference, that it really happened: and one must be content to accept it in the same way."* Suddenly his dulled senses were re-sharpened, and he took the first, faltering steps of his Spiritual Journey. It is a slow journey out of cynicism and joylessness; he doesn't pretend growth that is not yet his, so he still sounds sometimes like Archie Bunker. The havoc of spiritual abuse penetrates the deeper layers of the brain, and the healing demands time, love, patience, prayer and study. The questioning and challenging attitude which got him in trouble in his youth are now the lamp and the compass of his journey.

Godspeed, Gerry.

Please discuss the content of the article before considering the Reflection questions, Page 175.

Chapter IV – Knowledge for the Mind

Temptation

> ***Then Jesus was led up by the Spirit into the wilderness to be tempted by the devil.***
> ***(Matthew 4:1)***

I knew someone who, after quitting smoking, carried an opened pack of cigarettes for years, to remind himself that availability had nothing to do with it. I knew someone who cut up all his credit cards except American Express—the only one that wouldn't let him run up a balance. There is an old joke about a man walking into a bar and seeing a friend, obviously under the weather. He said: "Hey, Charlie—I thought your doctor was holding you to one drink a day." "Thash right," said Charlie: "And I'm being perfectly faithful. Now thish one here is for next July 26." I knew someone who joked: "I can resist anything except temptation!" I knew a lady, otherwise rational, who decided to limit herself to two cigarettes a day, instead of quitting altogether. Soon she was staying up until midnight and smoking the next day's "ration" before retiring. I knew a saintly man who said near the end of his life: "If there is any sin I have never committed, it was because I was never really tempted, or I feared the consequences."

How we do writhe in the face of temptation! "Why do we call it will-power?" someone asked. "It ought to be called won't-power." Bishop William Temple[50] has written: "If we try to be 'good' and to keep the rules of righteousness we shall fail, but if we see to it that the influence of Christ is stronger upon us every day we shall become not merely 'good' but partakers of the Divine Nature, co-operators with Christ in the redemption of the world, channels of the Holy Spirit"—as was Christ himself.

By contrast, when we call on will power, it appears to be mostly our own will, not God's, which is brought to bear. Do we not then risk replacing the resisted temptation with a worse sin—the deadly sin of pride? (Let's keep our terms straight here: pride in this sense does not mean a healthy dignity or self-respect; it is the haughty upstaging of God which traces back through the Tower of Babel to the expulsion from Eden.)

How did Jesus, fully tempted as we are (Hebrews 4:15) live a sinless life? Was he really "above all that?" Was it a kind of one-upmanship, to show that God was superior to man? Was he (as many through the centuries have claimed) not really Flesh and Blood, but just giving an appearance of humanity?

None of the above, I believe. He came to show us a better way. He lived perfectly in Love: not the warm-fuzzy love so appealing to us, but a Love willing to suffer, willing to die for the beloved. Thus the desire not to sin came from a motive bigger than temptation, bigger than will power. Once again we are confronted with the

Chapter IV – Knowledge for the Mind

topsy-turvy quality of the Laws of the Kingdom: the conquest of temptation comes not through resistance, but through surrender.

Please discuss the content of the article before considering the Reflection questions, Page 175.

Paul Stimson

The Language of the Kingdom

> *Truly I say to you, many prophets and righteous men longed to see what you see and did not see it, and to hear what you hear, and did not hear it.*
> *(Matthew 13:17)*

"Scrumptious salad!", you comment to your hostess. "Oh, just something I threw together," she replies, ever so casually. "Actually, I conjectured it," says she, after a pause. Studying the puzzled look on your face, she tries again: "Don't you understand? I just symbolized it!"

You smile faintly and start edging toward the door. She bursts into gales of laughter and leads you back to a chair. "Sorry to throw you off balance," she ventures, with a twinkle: "But last evening it struck me that the Latin *conjecture* and the Greek *symbol* have the same literal meaning: throw together! And it all seems to fit with what little I know about the mind-set of these Ancients: the legalistic, left-brained Romans assembling fragments of what they do know and conjecturing conclusions about the unknown, while the intuitive, right-brained Greeks used physical objects as symbols of their spirituality."

Chapter IV – Knowledge for the Mind

This points up the reason why there is not, and never will be, a single, definitive translation of the Bible—or anything else, for that matter. Language differences are not just a matter of having different words to mean the same thing; they represent entirely different cultural experiences and modes of thinking. If you look up certain words of the Bible in a Greek-English lexicon, you sometimes find that it takes a whole paragraph to convey the meaning—and perhaps inadequately, at that.

As if that were not enough trouble, different writers often differ markedly in their usage of words. The best example I can think of is the age-old belief that Paul and James had opposing theologies of faith and works. Where James wrote of works stemming from faith, Paul wrote of fruits of the Spirit. To Paul, works meant works of the Law, or trying to earn the free gift of Salvation by being good and doing good things. Paul was saying it couldn't be done, and James would not have disagreed.

But if you think all this is troublesome, try to grasp the breadth and depth of the problem Jesus faced, trying to convey a vision of the Kingdom of Heaven in any human tongue. We know nothing of the modes of communication in the Kingdom, let alone anything of the concept of language there. Jesus used a lot of similes, all striving to connect our experience in space-time to the unknowable otherness of what lies beyond: *"The Kingdom of Heaven is like treasure hidden in a field . . . like one pearl of great value . . . like a net thrown into the sea . . . " (Matthew 13:44-47)*. The numerous parables try to convey in a roundabout way, ideas which cannot be expressed directly. He said: In my Father's House are many rooms (or "mansions," in the King James Version). We can spend a lifetime trying to grasp what that means.

He also spoke of what is not: either-or issues may turn into both-and, or a third choice that we wouldn't have thought of. When some nitpicker tried to pin him down with a story about a woman widowed seven times, and whose wife she would be in Heaven, he made it clear that the question had no meaning (Matthew 22:23-33).

Hopelessly complex, it sometimes seems. Yet in one sentence, he brought it all within reach: *"He who has seen me has seen the Father" (John 14:9)*. How do we see Jesus? Mainly through reading the Bible and learning to see Reality through its pages.

Some days I can read a passage of Scripture and see only a jumble of words; the next day the same text may leap off the page. Gradually, I learn to grasp the Language of the Kingdom.

Please discuss the content of the article before considering the Reflection questions, Page 175.

Chapter IV – Knowledge for the Mind

Spoken Word, Written Word

...for it is not you who speak, but the Spirit of your Father speaking through you.
(Matthew 10:20)

To anyone who has given them a moment's thought, the spoken and written idioms are vastly different. On the one hand, listen to an unskilled reader of the printed page, singsong voice or no inflection at all, pausing mechanically at every mark of punctuation and eliding all in between. Then for contrast, try reading the transcribed text of a conversation.

The skilled writer and the accomplished speaker can bridge the worst of these gaps. Punctuation is for the eye, not the ear; a good reader will run right over some commas and insert pauses and inflections not indicated in the text. An alert writer will listen to the speakers' sentence structures and methods of supplying emphasis, and thus learn to hold the readers' attention. But some differences persist. Since a reader has the option of reviewing what went before, the writer is afforded complexity which would be lost on a listener. A speaker's ambience adds nuances not available to the writer.

I will amplify these thoughts with some notes from personal experience. I have often told the story of my father's speech defect, and its miraculous healing in his mid-twenties as his vocation to the priesthood was forming. Try as I might, I have never been able to get through the telling without choking up at the climax of the story. Not long ago I decided that the story deserved to live beyond my life span, so I wrote it. I was conscious at the time of writing that it came out in my written style, quite different from the oral idiom. I was startled, though, to note that I could read aloud the written version without any hint of choking up. Correspondingly, I am quite sure that the written version has had less impact on the reader or on the hearer as I read it aloud.

That realization was a major part of the motivation for writing this essay. As I edited and organized my book, it weighed on me all the more. Soon I saw the need for a total rewrite of my father's story; I started again without even looking at the earlier effort. This time I relied more on my father's own recollection of the events, weaving into it some of his first-person report. Now I choke when I read it, feeling older and wiser. It is Cleft Palate, page 10 of this book.

My limited experience of preaching presents another case in point. During the 1980s, when I was exploring my own sense of a vocation to ordination (which was never realized), my rector often let me preach to small gatherings, such as evening Eucharists on saints' days. I had a strong sense of inspiration, and quickly developed an extemporaneous style which, I dare to believe, worked well. Sometimes I came to it with a few keywords on a scrap of paper, and sometimes with no notes. But on two occasions during

Chapter IV – Knowledge for the Mind

those years I was given the Sunday morning pulpit, and simply did not dare to present that informal style before hundreds of people. For weeks in advance I cut and polished, word-by-word. The grammar, syntax, spelling, rationale, and implications for spiritual growth were as developed and refined as I could have made them, but try as I might; I could not bring those words to life as I floated them off the page and into the air. Total disaster; I should have stayed in bed.

I recall, too, that my father never read his sermons, but formed his words on the fly. He was as conscientious as any about sermon preparation, but occasionally scrapped his prepared notes a few minutes before he entered the pulpit and preached on something entirely different. These daring substitutions were noted as being among his best ever; inspiration operates by its own mysterious rules.

As I ponder the Holy Grail of word-smithing, suddenly pops into my head the Gettysburg Address[51] of Abraham Lincoln, which I was compelled to memorize in school years. Unlike Edward Everett's two-hour tedium which preceded it on the dais that day, these 239 words will live as long as civilization endures. Google it; read silently, then read it again aloud. In these 239 words I see the distinct qualities of written and spoken idiom as fusing into one; thus, the perfect oration lives on as the perfect essay.

Preachers and orators everywhere, please take note. Fumbles, stumbles, even the laughing-off of a lapse in a train of thought, are quickly forgotten, but spontaneity may convey impact to be remembered long after the words have faded.

Please discuss the content of the article before considering the Reflection questions, Page 176.

Reflection Questions: Chapter IV

Symbols of the Holy Trinity

1) Does understanding the human trinity of heart, soul and mind help to understand the Holy Trinity? Why or why not?
2) What images come to mind when you picture the Holy Trinity?
3) Do you lean on, pray to, or call upon one part of the Trinity more than the others?
4) Has your appreciation of each part of the Trinity changed as you have grown spiritually?

Our Worm's-Eye View of Reality

1) Think of and describe a time when you felt that your place in the Universe was insignificant.
2) Using analogy, simile or metaphor, how would you explain your unexplainable God to someone else?
3) 3"God is like ..."
4) Understanding your own human limitations, what is your personal perception of Heaven? Of afterlife?
5) What other concepts of your faith are you able or unable to visualize?

Time & Eternity

1) What is your perception of Eternity?
2) How does that perception influence your daily life?
3) Is eternity a long time, or is it "outside" the creation called "space-time"?
4) In earlier Christianity, God was seen as living on the top floor of a little three-story universe. But now, is the Creator within space-time, or "outside."? How far away is that?

The Spiritual Dimension

1) How comfortable are you with the understanding the the Kingdom of God is within you?
2) What part does faith play in realizing the Kingdom within you?
3) In what ways does that in dwelling manifest itself in your spiritual life?
4) What other illustrations might you use to explain this fourth and spiritual dimension to help others understand it?

5). What characteristics have you seen in yourself and others that are indicators of a fourth and spiritual dimension?

Either/Or Versus Both/And

1) How do you feel about living in a created universe? Living in a universe that created itself? What would be the advantages and disadvantages of either?

2) Would knowing the truth about creation change the way you live? How? Why?
3) What questions, if answered, would clarify your understanding of how the Universe came to be?
4) How comfortable are you with both/and? Why?

The Hebrew Scriptures

1) Have you experienced "Spiritual Abuse"? What do you think was the motivation of the abuser?
2) .Is it important for our "Salvation History" to include misdeeds done in the name of religion? Why or Why not?
3) Are there hurtful people who have turned your love to anger?
4) What will it take to love them again?

Temptation

1) What temptations are hardest for you to confront?
2) How might your triumph over those temptations further God's Kingdom on Earth?
3) Surrender: - The night he was betrayed, Jesus faced the temptation to chicken-out: "Father, if it be possible, let this cup pass from me. Nevertheless, your will be done."

The Language of the Kingdom

1) How tolerant are you of ambiguity and uncertainty—both in general and in matters of faith?

2) Are you able to share your understanding of faith with people who have different cultural values and experiences?
3) Jesus spent time with many different types of people. Ponder how differently his presence, words and actions affected them.
4) Many believe that the Father wants uncompromised obedience to his commandments. Others say that Love is uppermost. Can you resolve these?

Spoken Word, Written Word

1) Can you rephrase a paragraph of the Gettysburg address?
2) How does your copy compare to Lincoln's?
3) Were the Epistles of Paul to the churches meant to be read aloud to the people or read silently by the recipient?

Chapter V – Churchy Stuff

The title "Churchy Stuff" may sound flip, but it is not our purpose to make light of this essential subject. Rather, since it is hoped that some readers of this book are on the outside looking in, these articles have been clustered at the end.

Please do keep reading, and come on in. The quaint language will soon be old hat.

Paul Stimson

Vocation

> *...to equip the Saints for the work of ministry...*
> *(Ephesians 4:12)*

When Jesus needed twelve to journey with him (Mark 1:16ff and parallels), he didn't wait for them to sense "the call" and seek him out. Years later, when those twelve were in overload, they instructed the brethren to pick out seven from among them (Acts 6:1 –7), to be ordained the first deacons. The election of bishops has long followed the same pattern, with the clergy and people taking the initiative. Ambrose, Bishop of Milan in the 4th Century, was not yet baptized when the people proclaimed him bishop.

Somehow, the vocation to ordained ministry appears to have taken a different course through the centuries, being seen in most times and places as primarily a private matter between God and the individual. The Church's purview has ranged from nonexistent to perfunctory, often more concerned with seeing if there are any "why-nots" than looking for a "why."

We are finding a new balance: vocations are scrutinized as never before. An even more important feature is seen in our recent ordination of a deacon: while I'm sure that the ordinand's journey has had intensely personal elements, the sense that this congregation has raised him up is unmistakable, pointing as it does back to the pattern seen in Acts.

But the concept of a vocation to any lay ministry has been until now a rarity. As we move deeper into the process of being the Church, not just going to Church, the need for lay ministry can only increase. Often we prove better able to recognize gifts in each other than in ourselves. We also are good at seeing each other's weaknesses and blind spots—the things which interfere with ministry. Here we must wrestle with the command to speak the truth in love (Ephesians 4:15), holding it ever in tension with the suggestion that we remove the log from our own eye before going after the speck in another's.

Please discuss the content of the article before considering the Reflection questions, Page 223.

Opposing God?

> *Is it I, Lord?*
> *(Matthew 26:22)*

The Sanhedrin[52] had a problem that was as intractable as any they had ever faced, and the solution, in its startling lucidity, silenced all opposition. ". . .if this plan or this undertaking is of men it will fail," said Gamaliel. "But if it is of God you will not be able to overthrow them. You might even be found opposing God." (Acts 5:27 40.)

Gamaliel cited instances of wrongheadedness that had gone before, and in succeeding chapters of the Acts of the Apostles we see Saul of Tarsus, as fervently, ferociously off the mark as any has ever been. The Arian Heresy, the Crusades, the Inquisitions, were all single mindedly in the Name of God and for the purification of the Faith. Perhaps the current turmoil over sexual orientation will be seen in the same embarrassing light.

God has granted us a great gift: the capacity to think for ourselves, and to reinterpret the thoughts of those who have gone before. Whenever we exercise that talent to discern the Will of God, we can be sure that some will say "Right on!", some "Yeah, maybe," and some will threaten burning at the stake.

Chapter V – Churchy Stuff

In these modern times we must wrestle with issues that people of apostolic times could not have imagined. It should therefore come as a relief to see that one (or more?) of our perennial, vexing issues was definitively and for all time solved, way back then. Hear it again, folks: if it is not of God it will fall of its own weight, and will not need our help in bringing it down. The resolutions, the reconciliation, move in God's time, not ours. But our facile familiarity with the Scriptures can get in the way; it is tempting to say, "Oh yeah, that." and move on.

But who, me? Opposing God?

Please discuss the content of the article before considering the Reflection questions, Page 223.

Advent

> *A voice cries out: "In the wilderness prepare the way of the Lord, make straight in the desert a highway for our God... Then the glory of the Lord shall be revealed, and all people shall see it together, for the mouth of the Lord has spoken."*
> *(Isaiah 40:3,5)*

Year after year, Advent Sunday flutters across our path with little inner recognition in many of us. It is, in fact, New Year's Day on the Liturgical Calendar; I think we could at least throw a party. During the party we could point out, for example, the ending of Year B, the year of Mark, in the Principal Lectionary, and the start of Year C, the year of Luke. We could talk about the growing trend toward Advent altar hangings of blue, the color of Mary, instead of purple, the color of penitence and fasting. How do you feel about that?

At the risk of sounding cynical, I must say that I don't expect a lot of response to the question. This is not said for the purpose of making anyone feel guilty; it is to say, rather, that awareness of seasons and symbols runs in cycles. First we see a small, fervently devoted group who pass it on to their progeny, gradually losing a

Chapter V – Churchy Stuff

little of the fire at each transfer. In time all is lost but a hollow shell which is dutifully passed until a rebellious "sixties" generation puts it aside, for the betterment of all. The decaying old is fertile ground for the sprouting new.

People of all times and places have demonstrated that the anticipation of important events creates spiritual necessity for times of preparation. We hear of Native American rites of passage in which a young warrior is sent into the wilderness to expect a particular dream, and maintains a strict fast until it comes. Young medieval nobles kept a vigil before being knighted. Christian catechumens of the first few centuries were led through a period of prayer and fasting before their baptism at the Easter Vigil.

We see many of these advents throughout the Bible. Jacob had a night of wrestling with the angel of the Lord before his commissioning, signified by the change of his name to Israel. Elijah in the cave had to wait out the earthquake, wind and fire before finding the Lord in the still, small voice. Jonah saw God, the world and his mission in new light when he emerged from three days and nights in the belly of the whale. Saul of Tarsus, knocked to the ground and blinded, suffered the same, symbolic three days and nights in seclusion before the scales fell from his eyes—his outer sight restored and his inner sight reconstructed. Jesus himself undertook a monumental forty-day advent in preparation for his brief ministry among us, and demonstrated its continuing importance by a pattern of little advents, some in solitude and some with his disciples.

The social, secular distractions of the coming season are staggering. They contain Satan's effort to derail us, and God's call to devotion. In the already-but-not-yet perspective of the Kingdom of Heaven, every Advent is as big as the first Advent, when Mary and Joseph made their dutiful journey. There is simply no way around it: just as the Lent and Holy Week we keep determines the joy of Easter, so also the Advent we undertake determines the Christmas we celebrate.

Come to us, O blessed Jesus!

Please discuss the content of the article before considering the Reflection questions, Page 224

Chapter V – Churchy Stuff

Crisis in the Churches

> *...but you shall love your neighbor as yourself.*
> *I am the LORD.*
> *(Leviticus 19:18b)*

My first thought was a wish that the whole issue of sexual orientation would fade away: who needs this distraction from our ministry and mission? Close on its heels came the second thought: the recognition that this is our ministry and mission— without it, and the host of other social and spiritual issues in our midst, we would be back in Eden. Onward, Christian soldiers.

My first and strongest feeling, though, is one of revulsion: I simply don't understand how anyone could be aroused by another of the same sex. I state this bluntly because I believe it is the first and strongest feeling of many heterosexuals, and we will never get beyond that one, primordial feeling unless it is acknowledged openly.

Homosexuals maintain that their sexuality is not what they do, but who they are. I see no ground for disputing: who would accept a life of marginalization and persecution if there were an alternative? The debate about nature vs. nurture continues, and some claim cure, while others say that it is not a disease, so the concept of a cure is irrelevant.

Those who read the Bible as a rule book cite the same few verses ad nauseam; thus they claim a right to cherry-pick the rules that suit them—i.e. the rules that are no threat to themselves—and ignore the rest. Some of them may have at some time worked on the Sabbath; are they aware that by Exodus 35:2, they are under a sentence of death? Or that by Leviticus 11:10, the eating of shellfish is an abomination? No more football, because by Leviticus 11:6 –8, we are rendered unclean by touching the skin of a dead pig. And Leviticus 19:19 prohibits cotton-polyester blends.

Jesus was thoroughly versed in the Law. He is quoted as saying, "Not one iota of the Law shall pass away until all is accomplished." But have you noticed that, throughout his words and actions, Love trumps Law at every turn? Can you read the Acts of the Apostles without picking up this same thread—the one change that consistently affected these otherwise-clueless fishermen? These fledgling followers of the Way were accused of turning the world upside down (Acts 17:6b); looking back through the tunnel of time, we might better say that they got a good start on reverting the upside-down world. The one-and-only tool of their trade was Love.

Instead of the somewhat threadbare 'What would Jesus do?' Let us ask, "What would the Apostles have done?" They, like us, were mortal, fallible, sinful humans; they, too, were charged with forging a single way forward from diverse outlooks and attitudes. They sought and trusted the leading of the Holy Spirit, knowing full well that said Spirit does not speak out of both sides of his/her mouth. I see no sign that their process was in any sense democratic; rather, they weighed each other's views and sought unanimity. (Unanimity, at its roots, means of one spirit, or, in Christian usage, of one Spirit.).

Majority rule is probably the best we can do in our secular dealings, but the Kingdom of Heaven surely is not a democracy, and we need to learn to live by its Laws so we will not be strangers when we get there. All too readily we equate the majority opinion with the Will of God, and strife rules our deliberations. Let us take off the hobnailed boots and start listening to minority views.

The most intense controversy focuses on the ordination of homosexuals. Here, our opinion should not matter in the slightest. Why are we not, instead, inquiring God's Will in the matter? (Yes, some of the strident voices in opposition are confident that is exactly what they are doing, as are a number of strident voices that support. They just use different Bible quotes!) In the tortuous process leading to ordination, let our leaders put their major focus on one question: is the applicant's sense of God's call authentic? It has been wisely said that God does not choose those who are fit; rather, he fits those whom he has chosen. Beyond that, it is perilous to nit-pick report cards, résumés and revelations.

Please discuss the content of the article before considering the Reflection questions, Page 224.

Paul Stimson

Evangelism

> *"Thy Kingdom come; thy will be done,*
> *on earth as it is in Heaven."*
> *(Matthew 6:10)*

Decades ago I served a term on the governing body of my church, in which I, chairman of Special Events, was grateful that I had a definable task and measurable goals. The time was the mid-to-late eighties, when there was a lot of talk about the forthcoming Decade of Evangelism (the decade of the 1990s), and fitful efforts at preparing for it. We decided to assign *two* members to the Evangelism Commission. They groped, they agonized, and not much came of it. Perhaps that was predictable: to my perception, not much has come of that heralded Decade. My hunch is that by their very nature, such efforts are individual and function at gut level. Perhaps leaders in this sector need to spend less effort on planning, organizing and cheerleading, and more on witnessing and storytelling.

At the individual level I see much alertness and caring in my present congregation. Visitors are greeted warmly; if they show signs of being unfamiliar with the Episcopal liturgy, books are handed to them, open to the right page. We introduce ourselves and

Chapter V – Churchy Stuff

invite them to a coffee hour. Also, I think most of us wonder occasionally, "What ever happened to Clarence and Charlotte," and in a few instances go so far as to call and say, "We've missed you; how are you?"

I have long been aware that leadership has been lacking in such matters, and have known that I *should* take some initiative. I have been hindered by faltering faith, fearing to launch something I don't know how to do. I have let myself get ensnared in bureaucratic thinking, wondering just where Evangelism borders Pastoral Care on the one side, and Outreach on the other.

We need to keep coming back to the recognition that evangelism has much more to do with our *being* than with our *doing*. I am still in awe of an experience a few years ago in which a couple told me that their son, who rarely came to church, had been deeply moved by something I said to him, and was still speaking of it some months later. I couldn't say it to them, but must admit that I couldn't recall even meeting their son, much less having spoken to him, much less what I said. I kept wishing I could rewind and replay the tape; if it was such a jewel I need to tattoo it on my wrist so I can use it again and again. I know, though, that it was *not* a jewel: it was merely the right thing at the right time. It was Spirit-led, and it was a throwaway. (I planted, Apollos watered, but God gave the increase.)

I recommend the *Caring Evangelism*[53] program, which teaches that "People don't care what you know until they know that you care." It also teaches that in evangelism, the first task is evangelizing the evangelists. Jesus knew that; in those three years he said repeatedly, " . . . and do you still not understand?" They didn't; they couldn't. He commanded that they lay low and await the infilling of the Holy Spirit. They did. They learned that all else in their lives was enhanced, not diminished, when it was made secondary to the Great Commission, that they go and make disciples of all nations.

What happened next has been given to us as hindsight, far surpassing any foresight within the grasp of that ragged band. We must keep asking: will that hindsight be to us an advantage or a hindrance?

Please discuss the content of the article before considering the Reflection questions, Page 224.

Peter & Paul

> *There is neither Jew nor Greek, there is neither slave nor free, there is neither male nor female; for you are all one in Christ Jesus.*
> *(Galatians 3:28)*

Peter and Paul are the only Saints who are commemorated twice in our liturgical calendar. We celebrate The Confession of St. Peter on January 18. (Confession, as used here, has nothing to do with owning up to wrongdoing. Rather, it means acknowledgment of belief or faith.) A week later, on January 25, we mark the Conversion of St. Paul. (Acts 9:3ff.) Then on June 29 we hold a joint celebration, The Feast of St. Peter and St. Paul.

In recent times the week that begins with the confession of Peter and spans the conversion of Paul has come to be called the Week of Prayer for Christian Unity. The reason for selecting that week for this purpose is not at all obvious; in fact, when we plumb the relationship between these two pioneers of The Way, we see many clues that they did not work together, and probably they were not best friends. In the first dozen chapters of the Acts of the Apostles the major focus is the ministry of Peter; Paul appears only as Saul, persecuting "heretics," then encountering the Risen Christ on

Damascus Road. The remaining chapters of Acts are dominated by Paul, with Peter making cameo appearances.

In the second chapter of the Letter to the Galatians, Paul reports a major confrontation with Peter. At issue was the spread of the Christian Gospel into the Gentile world, without which the fledgling Christian movement would have remained a Jewish sect, and might not have survived. In this as in all the tense episodes of Scripture, it is vital that we learn to look beyond the issues of who was right and who was wrong, so that we may perceive the Spirit of Truth making use of the contributions of both. (And if we can extend this understanding to ourselves and those around us, our lives will turn at once more productive and more tranquil.)

The battleground, actually, was far larger than just Peter and Paul. Some believed that Gentile converts must first subscribe to all the rites and practices of Judaism; Paul saw it otherwise. Paul's criticism of Peter was largely for his vacillating between the two.

Paul was the acknowledged "winner." I like to think that Peter's perspective was more ecumenical. The Jerusalem faction was right in calling attention to our roots in Judaism, but erred in trying to give it the force of law. Paul's "victory" probably contributed to the later forgetfulness of our origins, even to the point of persecuting Jews for having killed the Christ.

Later still, the use of the Hebrew Scriptures faded out, thus eradicating our sense of connectedness with God's Chosen People, our spiritual ancestors. When we ignore this record of Salvation History, we cannot grasp the failure of Law to save us. The coming of the Christ is then reduced to sentimental pap, or the ultimate Celestial Folly.

Peter and Paul are ideal role models in our quest for unity, not just in Christendom, but with all peoples. For all their differences of temperament and theology, they knew that their bond was unbreakable. They knew that the forces binding them together were far stronger than the divisive tensions. Would that we could frame our disagreements in such Grace.

Please discuss the content of the article before considering the Reflection questions, Page 225.

Paul Stimson

Beans & Rice

> *Breathe through the heats of our desire*
> *thy coolness and thy balm;*
> *Let sense be dumb, let flesh retire;*
> *speak through the earthquake, wind and fire,*
> *O still, small voice of calm.*
> *(John Greenleaf Whittier)*[54]

Long before the world knew what a nutritionist was, primitive peoples were busy learning and practicing good nutrition. The unfathomable complexity of the human organism demands a wide variety of foodstuffs to develop to its fullest, but has learned to make do with less wherever scarcity (or simply taste and distaste) shortens the menu.

Modern science has learned that proteins, essential for building body tissues, are made up of building blocks called amino acids. Of the large variety of these available in things we can eat, just eight amino acids are considered essential. Guess what: rice contains a full measure of some of these eight and beans contain a full measure of others, but it takes a mixture of the two to make complete protein. In parts of the world where survival is difficult, people long ago

Chapter V – Churchy Stuff

learned to eat both of these, and to eat them together. There are, of course, many other ways to attain good nutrition, but somehow this one is, to me, bedrock.

So it is with spiritual nutrition. The breakdown into followers of this or that, and the fragmenting of Christendom into denominations, seems to be marked more by what people deny than what they embrace. So we are at risk of spiritual malnutrition in midst of God's abundant gifts. (The Reformation was a squabble over authority. "We have tradition and an infallible Pope so we are right" "We have an infallible Bible so we are right." Both sides lost the balance.)

We are tempted, of course, to conclude that we Anglicans have the balanced diet, and that all the others are more-or-less malnourished. For many years I believed just that, but in the course of drifting away for ten long years and groping my way back "home," I have learned much from people of other persuasions. There is much we may garner by seeing ourselves through their eyes.

Two of my close friends were brought up as Quakers. Drawn by the Sacraments and the richness of our liturgy, they later became Episcopalians. Our Creeds and Articles of Religion, etc. were a shock to them, but they are struggling toward a mature faith with the rest of us. The notable fact is that they have brought with them the greatest richness of their upbringing, which is the spiritual power of silence. Yes, in social situations they are both "motor mouths," but the spiritual side of them knows how to listen in silence, and to speak when they believe the Spirit speaks through them. In my perception they have the beans and the rice, and I struggle to gain what they have.

I will risk a giant leap from this small observation and suggest that Anglicanism and Quakerism are the beans and rice of Christendom. When we hear of Elijah in the cave (I Kings 19:9 ff), we feel the intensity of his finding God in the still, small voice. Every time the Sacraments are celebrated, we hope and pray that Quakers will be drawn to share with us the awe, the majesty and the mystery.

Please discuss the content of the article before considering the Reflection questions, Page 225.

Chapter V – Churchy Stuff

Loaves & Fishes

> ...*And Elisha said, "Give to the men, that they may eat." But his servant said, "How am I to set this before a hundred men?" So he repeated, "Give them to the men that they may eat, for thus saith the Lord, ' They shall eat and have some left.' "*
> *(2Kings 4:42)*

At a conference of small parishes, I sat at dinner with three ladies who felt that their parish would close its doors within a few years. I estimated that they were all well along in years; they described themselves as the "young" contingent of the parish. They felt that they had really tried to be outgoing, but no younger people were coming in.

The next morning I attended a workshop on Christian Education, and listened to two ladies from two different parishes, both of which had been in the same predicament a few years before. Both congregations had "turned the corner," and by remarkably similar means. The story of one of these ladies seemed to me especially vivid: there had been no Sunday School for years; she started one by bringing in her own unchurched grandchildren, who brought with them one friend. Soon the kids brought in other friends, then persuaded their parents to come. The future seems assured.

Reflecting on this, I thought of loaves and fishes. "You give them something to eat," said Jesus. In at least one of the Gospel versions, a disciple balks at the prohibitive cost of bread for so many. But the crowd was large indeed; I have little doubt that by passing the hat, they would have been able to collect the 200 denarii. All would then have eaten their fill, but there would have been no story to write.

People have long speculated on what it was that really happened. Does God reserve the right to violate the Laws of Physics (his own Laws, mind you) by spilling lox and bagels out of the sky? Did most of the people just happen to have a little food with them? How easily we do miss the point! For our purposes here and today, the physics of the event matters not at all; rather, Jesus was telling us to start with who we are, where we are and what is at hand and expect miracles.

It is tempting indeed to settle into a belief that there are a gifted few who are called to be the instrument of extraordinary change, be it the reviving of a dying parish, or—dare we to breathe the suggestion— bringing a lost sheep into the fold. Our excuses are at the ready: ...don't know how . . . not confident enough in my own faith . . . what if they ask a question I can't answer?...evangelists are pushy . . . no time or energy for it.

Only two things we need: the knowledge that we are called, and the know-how to respond. To all who will wrestle earnestly with the

Chapter V – Churchy Stuff

Gospel message, the calling is inescapable—but don't leave home without it. The learning-how then becomes possible. Expect a miracle!

Please discuss the content of the article before considering the Reflection questions, Page 225.

Tithing

> *Bring the full tithes into the storehouse, that there may be food in my house; and thereby put me to the test, says the Lord of hosts, if I will not open the windows of heaven for you and pour down for you an overflowing blessing.*
> *(Malachi 3:10.)*

Why do people swim in cold water? The answer seems to be that it feels good, once we are wet all the way. And there are two ways of getting wet: wading in, an inch at a time, or taking the plunge. Wading works pretty well at first, but beyond waist-deep, it is agony.

I was for many years waist-deep into Stewardship. I had read and heard, over and over, the Biblical imperative on tithing, but couldn't force myself to advance beyond inch-at-a-time. Finally, and quite impulsively, I decided that God is faithful in his promises and I took the plunge more than twenty years ago.

I soon saw that I was living better on 90% of my income than I had been on 97% or 98%. I am always one to look for rational explanations; it may be that in newfound wisdom I was spending more thoughtfully, thus wasting less. But the how-and-why is not of first importance: God does move in mysterious ways, and my need to understand gradually faded.

But there was one persistent problem: every time I received an appeal for charity I had to wrestle through it anew. The current solution for me has been to give half the tithe to the Church, and the other half to a special fund which I consider to be already spent, so it is in joy, not stress, that I respond to the call for charity.

I see this not as a settled solution, but a work-in-progress. I offer it as a suggestion for those who, like me, struggle on the Journey. There are many among us who offer the full tithe, and still find their cups full to overflowing.

God is full of surprises, and loves a cheerful giver. Take the plunge: you'll be so glad you did.

Please discuss the content of the article before considering the Reflection questions, Page 226.

Paul Stimson

Big Ministries, Little Ministries

Whoever is faithful in a very little is faithful also in much . . .
(Luke 16:10)

It is easy to lose track of just how "new" the idea of Lay Ministry is in the life of the Church. I put "new" in quotes because it really is very old, but got lost for hundreds of years. With the feeling that it is a new thing goes the idea that we have a lot of work to do to prepare for it, and must face up to some major changes of lifestyle: sacrifices is the word that comes quickly to mind.

The biggest danger is actually the direct opposite of this: we pass up opportunities daily because they look small—just too small to bother with. Why take the time, the trouble, the risk when probably nobody will be noticeably better off for it? We might even blunder and do harm. This is what we are likely to think if we get up to the point of thinking about it. But we don't always get even that far.

Further, we often think of ministry as restricted to the ordained ministry. The clergy people have the ministry. We are the recipients (with perhaps a mutter that we pay for that ministry).

Chapter V – Churchy Stuff

This type of congregation has been likened to a football game: 22 people on the field in urgent need of rest and 22,000 people in the stands with urgent need for exercise. In God's eyes, we all have been gifted for a vocational ministry. We had better discover our unique gifts and get on with our ministry.

A key feature of ministry opportunities is that often they grow out of adversity—things not going the way we think they should. This is the very feature that reveals the hand of God, with its boundless capacity to turn events inside out.

Recent history provides a fine illustration. At a time when there was a shortage of funds, a regional grouping could no longer afford its former newsletter format as a wraparound on the national publication. They could not even afford postage, so chose the inelegant solution of distributing to the parishes in bundles.

But wait: here comes the hand of God, turning it inside out. The first step is that it is ever so easy to pass out copies to those who come to Church on the first Sunday of the month. From time to time we talk about reaching out to those who do not come regularly, or who are absent because of illness or other misfortune, but it is hit-or-miss. We have no systematic way of noticing who comes and who doesn't.

Aha: obviously we must label all copies first so we will know who got it and who didn't. The leftover pile is the "didn't" list. If these were quickly sorted by neighborhoods, people could pick up a few which are addressed to near neighbors during Coffee Hour and drop them off on the way home, saying simply, "Hello, how are you, we missed you." Those not taken can still be mailed, of course. (One caution: if you mail in a postal class that requires a minimum number of copies, hold back that number.)

You know the obstacles as well as I do. It's not really our job or vocation, it seems too small a thing to bother with, and we'd really rather just get home and read the Sunday paper. And some people might actually be annoyed, or embarrassed.

But can you know that if you haven't tried it?

Please discuss the content of the article before considering the Reflection questions, Page 226.

Truth

> *Pilate asked: "What is truth?"*
> *(John 18:38)*

Pontius Pilate was profoundly perplexed. Standing before him was Jesus Christ, whose very presence laid bare the decades of lies which enveloped not only the life of Pilate, but the entire culture that had formed him. Who was this Man whose "wrong-doing" was such a threat to his own half-baked sense of "right"?

Probing around the edges, and terrified of the impending collapse of his world, poor pagan Pontius tried to temporize: "So you are a king?" Jesus replied: "...For this I was born, and for this I have come into the world, to bear witness for the truth. Everyone who is of the truth hears my voice." Pilate stood naked in the Light: "What is truth?", he quavered. The rest of the dialog, if in fact any more was said, is lost to history. Thus, the question lies ever fresh before us.

What is truth? If we dare to keep asking, our lives are transformed. But nowhere is the question more critical than when we witness to our Faith. If I come to you proclaiming the love of Christ, and my real motive is getting you into the pew behind me so

I can help balance our budget and feel good about church growth, you are probably going to know it and reject me. That is the best outcome, for it witnesses to Truth. We have a worse outcome if your rejection of me leads you into the falsehood of rejecting Christ. But the outcome is worst possible if you buy into my lie, so the infection spreads. I see this as the great tragedy of some practitioners of the Electronic Church, who know enough of our evasion of Truth to bring us to our knees—right in front of our checkbook.

What is truth? The truth is that, this side of the Kingdom, we will never get it right. I am painfully aware that everything I say and do stems from mixed motives. But I must keep reminding myself that it is OK, simply because that is the way God made me. God uses everything. We see ' . . . through a glass darkly,' but at least we have the glass. If we all knew Truth, what need would there be for anyone to witness it?

Evangelism, the Great Commission to which we were pledged in our baptismal vows, must be undertaken in full awareness of the ulterior motive, which is church growth. The paradox is that ulterior motives cannot simply be dismissed; they can be neutralized only by being brought to the surface. Would you buy a car from a salesman who insists that his only motive for steering you from that 'good' car to this 'better' car is love for you and concern for your well-being?

I believe that our faltering, tremulous approach to evangelism can prosper if we stop seeing it as an individual duty and a denominational movement. In the divided Church of this broken world, we must see our differences—the very differences which are our excuse for alienation—as God's gifts to us. The more diversity (and its acceptance) in the community, the more we look like the Kingdom of Heaven. None of us is as smart as all of us. An ecumenical approach to evangelism can cross cultural and political boundaries, learning first to ignore those boundaries and eventually to obliterate them. Let us get out into our neighborhoods, confer with the pastors and elders of nearby churches, establish dialog with political leaders. Remember that our commission is simply to witness to God's Truth, not to convert, not to shame—always offering a choice, as Jesus did, and always respecting God's gift of free will. Tell God's Truth and leave conversion to the Holy Spirit—who does it far better than we can.

Look at it this way: in our fallen state, Truth is simply too big for our embrace. We glimpse it through keyholes. Any two keyholes will always reveal more than one.

Please discuss the content of the article before considering the Reflection questions, Page 226.

Paul Stimson

Interfaith Relations

*You shall know the truth,
and the truth will make you free.
(John 8:32)*

We all are seekers of truth: who in his right mind would contest that? But let that quest collide with one of our Sacred Cows, and watch the fireworks. I think it was Josh Billings who remarked that ignorance is problem enough, but the stuff we "know" that isn't so is a far worse hindrance.

Ptolemy, Hero of Alexandria and Copernicus all understood that the Earth is round, yet the near-universal belief in flat Earth persisted for centuries. Some people believe that a blanket or a sweater is a source of heat, not merely an insulator, and will try to warm a cold, inanimate object by wrapping it.

These examples pertain to physical facts where opinion should have no bearing, yet we must deal with the reality, which is that opinion rules. Fault our educational system; sputter, rant and rave as you wish, but the fact remains that we live in a poor climate for keeping fact and opinion in their assigned corners.

Polite society warns us that politics, sex and religion are forbidden subjects, and we override that warning at our peril. But in

Chapter V – Churchy Stuff

2006, 138 Muslim scholars saw the necessity of breaking a logjam, and they issued an invitation to dialog with Christians. There have been many responses to that invitation, and as a result, numerous small groups have drawn Muslims and Christians into dialog.

For perspective, it is of value to pause here and remind ourselves that there are in this world not two but three major monotheistic religions. Christianity has for many centuries ignored, largely, its roots in Judaism. Genesis, Psalms and Proverbs have long been popular, but not until the latter years of the 20th Century did main-line Christian liturgies include a significant contribution from the Hebrew Scriptures. It is plain to see that Islam has roots in Christianity (thus ultimately in Judaism), but it appears to this observer that this lineage is only reluctantly acknowledged by Muslims. Most important, the emotional tension between Muslims and Jews is extreme. The animosity is more political than theological; still, the prospect for productive, three-way discussion seems remote —for the foreseeable future, at least. This is why the current focus is on Muslim-Christian dialog.

The 138 Muslim scholars wisely chose to focus initially on what they have in common with Christianity, rather than pressing our differences. The central theme in our discussions has been the command to love God, and to love our neighbor as we love ourselves. We soon saw that healthy love of self cannot be assumed, and we have work to do before love of self and of neighbor can blend harmoniously.

In the small group attended by this writer, significant friendships have formed: at the start of each meeting, it can be seen that the participants are truly glad to see each other. This all by itself would make the meetings worthwhile; if millions of such small groups were to form and to share this experience, the effect on worldwide political climate would be dramatic.

Is that a realistic possibility? Sorry if I am jolting any dreamers awake, but it must be noted that the people now engaging in these dialogs are a slender, self-selected minority. We are educated people and we are caring people, and those two qualities do not automatically combine. The gratifications we have experienced will not readily spread to many others, but we must remember that our call is to faithfulness, and that does not mean we are required to be successful. God's Holy Spirit, and whatever is its equivalent in Muslim theology, is responsible for the results.

So where do we go from here? Surely the dialogs must continue. But can it forever be peaches and cream? Do we not have an ultimate duty to dig deep enough to discover where there are parallel truths that can comfortably coexist, and what Sacred Cows must be sacrificed on the Altar of Truth? On both sides?

This writer here enters into rocky terrain, expressing a troubling conclusion that has gradually come into focus in nearly two years of talks. The initial choice to focus on the command to love God and neighbor was wise, but a vital discrepancy comes into view:

The central message of Jesus, God the Son, is that God loves his Creation and all its creatures. The scriptural basis for this belief starts in the creation story in Genesis, where at the end of each Day, "God saw that it was good." There is much in the Hebrew Scriptures that reinforces the image of a vengeful God, but much of that seems to echo the feelings of a small boy who has done wrong and is expecting a whipping. Isaiah's four Servant Songs, pointing to a Savior willing to suffer for our sake, are a weighty counterpoise to that view. The ensuing message of Jesus is distilled in the later epistles of John, not merely that God loves us, but that God is Love.

The word, Islam, translates as submission. This writer hears the Muslims acknowledge the command to love Allah; they speak of the Power of Allah, the Justice of Allah, the Mercy of Allah, but never a word of the Love of Allah. This is troubling because of my belief, gradually, painfully gained, that Love is a two-way street, and no one-way version of it even exists. All the talk in literature, fiction and non-fiction alike, of unrequited love is illusory. Desire, longing, lust are one-way streets; love blossoms when the connection is completed. Submission in a one-way love feels dangerous. When the Angel Gabriel dictated the Qur'an to Mohammed, how is it that he neglected to mention that Allah loves us, one and all, with a steadfast, unconditional love, and His fondest hope is that we will spread it around to each other and to His Creation, while reflecting some of it Heavenward?

Make no mistake: submission is a vital element of love. Bilateral submission is a foundation stone in person-person love but, sadly, it is rarely attained. But can we even imagine God in submission to humankind? The startling answer is that He does just that: He even sent His Son, His only Son to deliver the Good News, knowing full well that we would not tolerate the Light of Truth and the Heat of Love.

The Christian is taught that love "is patient and kind, not jealous or boastful, not arrogant or rude. Love does not insist on its own way; it is not irritable or resentful; it does not rejoice at wrong, but rejoices in the right. Love bears all things, believes all things, hopes all things, endures all things." (I Corinthians 13:4-7) We are perfect, right? No, God knows that we are but dust (Psalm 103:14). Individually and collectively we commit atrocities. The Crusades and the Inquisitions could never have happened if we had been paying attention. There is some evidence that we are paying attention now better than before. It is to be hoped that we will not repeat those sins, but we have new possibilities ever before us.

The key message is that love is ever at the center of all, and absolutely the only worthy motive for all thought, word and action.. When Saul of Tarsus, fervently believing that he was doing God's will, set about to eradicate the people of The Way, some surely were tempted to hatch a plot against him and get him out of the way. But love prevailed; it was the soul-searing love of God that brought him to his knees, and made him Paul the Apostle, a key figure in the spread of Christianity to all nations.

Please discuss the content of the article before considering the Reflection questions, Page 227.

Chapter V – Churchy Stuff

The E Word

> *And he who sat upon the throne said:*
> *"Behold, I make all things new."*
> *(Revelation 21:5a)*

"I'm offended," said my questioner, "by strangers knocking on my door and pushing a religion I'm not interested in. And you are asking me to go out and do that to other strangers?" In the few recent months I have been speaking here and there around the Diocese, I have been amazed at the intensity of the opposition to my words about evangelism—a term which stirs negative feelings in many of us. "We need to reclaim the word," someone recently remarked.

We need to reclaim the word. Evangelism needs not, should not be pushy, simply because God is not pushy. (A pushy God would not even need evangelists!) We must remember in this, as in all communication, that tone of voice, body language, timing and choice of words profoundly affect the perceived message. It is not an act we can put on: the reality of who we are and what we are feeling will be seen. God asks only that we be real.

We need to reclaim the word. Evangelism rarely has anything to do with strangers who remain strangers, because God is intensely personal and intimate. In making friends of strangers we can first find, then speak to, their need, their hope, their pain. The very God who has the hairs of our heads numbered could never take a one-size-fits-all approach to us. It therefore must never be a hit-run event, leading people to a conversion prayer then setting them adrift to be blown about by every wind of change. Months or years of spiritual milk must provide nurture to the point where solid food can be taken. Evangelism needs to be followed by loving mentoring in the shared faith. It's not, "and then they accepted Jesus and lived happily ever after, and I hung another scalp from my belt or put another notch in my spiritual six-gun."

We need to reclaim the word. Evangelism does not count heads. Since disappointment is the cause of burnout, we must not even look for "results." Ours is to speak faithfully the Word of God, knowing that only the Holy Spirit can convert. Thus, evangelism is not a thing we need to get out and start doing: it is something we already are doing, consciously or not. Every time a friend expresses to us a joy or a sorrow, a pain or a blessing, our response conveys our knowledge and love of God, be it a dimly burning wick or a light that overcomes darkness. Our great commission is merely to get more intentional and better focused about it.

Please discuss the content of the article before considering the Reflection questions, Page 227.

Chapter V – Churchy Stuff

The Governance of the Church[55]

> *Have this mind among yourselves,*
> *which is yours in Christ Jesus.*
> *Philippians 2:5)*

Part I: the Unanimity Rule

Winston Churchill[56] once said that Democracy is the worst form of government in the world, except for all the others. We plod along in a largely democratic governance of the Church, ignoring clear evidence that the Kingdom of Heaven never was and never will be a Democracy. I believe that we are here to learn the Laws of the Kingdom, so that we will not be strangers when we get there.

I am quite sure that the Holy Spirit does not speak out of both sides of his/her mouth. Governing mandates of 51% vs. 49%—and even closer—are commonplace in the democratic process. Worse still are the cases when "consensus" is really a 40% to 35% to 25% plurality. Majorities—and even pluralities—have a bad habit of trampling on minorities, and going to devious lengths to maintain the lead.

The small number of churches which have dared to establish and abide by a rule of unanimity have had, in all cases of which I am aware, startlingly wonderful experiences. When one lone nay vote can block an overwhelming majority, the way people think about each other and treat each other changes profoundly. Suddenly, the minority view is truly heard—and occasionally turns out to be the better perspective. The classic movie, Twelve Angry Men, vividly portrays a jury trial in which an initial 11 –1 vote for conviction comes gradually, agonizingly around to 0 –12, and an acquittal. Thanks be to God for the unanimity rule in criminal cases.

In a parish to which I belonged for many years, the governing body had long operated by the rule of unanimity. The decision to make that change was, as you might expect, a difficult one—it was necessarily a unanimous decision. (Think about the very word unanimous, which simply means of one spirit, or, in Christian usage, of one Spirit).

There came a time when all three furnaces in the church buildings gave out at once. They squeaked through the waning days of winter, then let the matter drift: why patch the roof on a sunny day? But come September it was clear that New England's harsh winter was soon upon them, and they addressed the problem.

There was a three-way division of opinion as to who should get the contract, and compelling reasons to back the arguments. One of the three contenders was soon ruled out by unanimous consent, but the proceedings deadlocked there. They trusted the process they had committed to, and left it unresolved. In the following weeks they did their homework, interviewing both contractors. It wasn't much talked about, but I am quite sure they devoted prayer time to the issue.

Chapter V – Churchy Stuff

By the time of the October meeting, with chill already in the air, they were of one mind. The contract was fulfilled before any pipes froze. After that, no one doubted that the process had served them well. Had it all been done by the more common majority rule, the losers would no doubt have been trying to build a new coalition to win the next one, and could scarcely have restrained a gentle I told you so if the chosen system had not met expectations.

The national and international governing bodies of many denominations seem unable to get past their squabbles over issues which are not trivial, but which should not be allowed to occupy center stage. I do not wonder that it is so; I wonder more that the democratic approach works as well as it does. To me, trying to bring in the Kingdom of Heaven by majority rule is rather like trying to make vichyssoise without potatoes.

I hear thunderous objections, of course. The first major convention adopting such a rule might pass not a single resolution. To this I can only say Alleluia! We would then be well on our way toward coming to grips with what Paul had in mind when he wrote: ...complete my joy by being of the same mind, having the same love, being in full accord and of one mind. (Philippians 2:2). Perhaps the individual Churches will lead the way from the bottom up.

Please discuss the content of the article before considering the Reflection questions, Page 227.

Part 2: The "High Five"

Further experience with the Unanimity Rule has revealed a flaw in its practice: an enthusiastic faction can overwhelm a quiet, thoughtful minority, putting them in a position where they simply do not feel like presenting a contrasting view. A vivid (and tragic) example of this has been noted in the political scene; long after the failed 1961 invasion of Cuba's Bay of Pigs, it was reported that some participants in the planning harbored serious misgivings, but feared ridicule from the ardent, overconfident promoters of the attack.

A similar problem has been reported from a Church which had long used the rule, and there is reason to believe that it can happen anywhere. A more nuanced version of the rule has been tried, and shows promise of solving the problem. In the High Five version, the simple "yea" or "nay" is replaced by the numbers one through five, with the following meanings:

- Five means, "It sounds great; I am all for it."
- Four means, "It sounds OK and I see no problems, but I am not enthusiastic."
- Three means, "I have serious misgivings, but will not stand in the way."
- Two means, "I feel that we do not have enough information to proceed with this."
- One means, "I believe this would be a grave mistake, and I cannot let it happen."

In the terms of the rule, Two and One are blocking votes, effectively a veto. (The blocking effect of a Two should be understood to be temporary, pending the gathering of the missing information.) While not strictly required under the rule, it is urged that any Three vote be examined with some care before moving on. Never forget that an unpopular view is not necessarily in error!

The adoption of a unanimity rule is a serious commitment, and not to be entered into lightly. It should be obvious that it could be adopted only by a unanimous vote. But the High Five modification presents an interesting possibility: the votes one through five could be substituted for yea and nay without any commitment to apply the terms of the rule. It would serve a valuable purpose in helping people understand each other's thinking. Let us bear in mind that in Church polity we should shun the win-lose mind-set that dominates the political scene. Rather, it is our aim to discover and implement the Will of God, and there is no such thing as a loser in that quest.

Please discuss the content of the article before considering the Reflection questions, Page 228.

Paul Stimson

Powers of Two

> *All authority in heaven and on earth has been given to me. Go therefore and make disciples of all nations, baptizing them in the name of the Father and of the Son and of the Holy Spirit, teaching them all that I have commanded you; and lo, I am with you always, to the close of the age.*
> *(Matthew 28:18b –20)*

You may have heard a fable about a beachcomber who was seen on the ebb tide one morning, picking up starfish stranded at the high-water mark and tossing them into the sea. "Why do you waste your time on those worthless creatures?" asked a bystander: "And besides, there are countless millions of them—what difference do you think you can make?" "Made a difference to that one," replied the beachcomber, as the next starfish splashed into the water. The first question was answered by the glow on the beachcomber's face.

If that tale moves you, even a little, you are ready to hear the paradox, which is that we are not in the business of counting cost or measuring results as we work for the coming of the Kingdom, yet we need to know that the task is not hopeless.

Chapter V – Churchy Stuff

Suppose you, all by yourself, made prayerful commitment to share your experience of the Christian Faith with just two people in the coming year, bringing them to such fervor that they would offer the same vow: to bring two more apiece into the Fold. The rest of the bargain is that you, then, have fulfilled your lifetime duty, and you can sit back and watch the action.

Two in the first year and four in the second; that is painfully slow. Eight, sixteen, thirty-two: visible if it all happened in one small parish, but otherwise lost in the noise. At the ten-year mark, one thousand—still a drop in the global bucket. Twenty years, one million: hey, we've been noticed. Thirty years, one billion—we're on a roll.

By the best reckoning of our scholars, our Lord dwelt among us thirty-three years. In the thirty-third year of this sequence, which you started back in 2008, the count passes the eight-billion mark. Since there are only about five billion of us, we are nearly through second helpings for all.

Two small cautions: the first is that you (like me, like the rest of us) have some work to do: your two prospects will probably not respond to your teaching or your urging, but to the Light that shines in your life, and your relationship has to be such that they will see and experience that light. The second is that when you have done your dutiful two, you will no way be able to sit and watch.

OK, there are two flaws in the argument: it has taken you more than one year to reach such spiritual maturity that your unchurched neighbors would notice, and maybe another year to develop the relationship of a respected friend. And the same will be true of them. (Someone once commented that new Christians should be put in the deepfreeze for six months!). So maybe it takes five, ten times as long? Second, our Lord set a key example when he sent the Seventy out two by two. There is no rule against going alone, but often it seems to go better in pairs, in teams.

Time's a-wastin'.

Please discuss the content of the article before considering the Reflection questions, Page 228.

Reflection Questions, Chapter V

Vocation

1) Have you ever experienced a "call" from God? If so, share your experience. If not, why do you think that is so?
2) Are there gaps in the ministry of your congregation? How can you help fill them?
3) Make a list of the gifts God has given you. Are you sharing all of them with his people?

Opposing God

1) How can you sense if you are working for or against the will of God?
2) What habits promote a too-facile familiarity with the Scriptures?
3) Give examples of instances when something you were working on failed because it wasn't in sync with God's will
4) Remember that when Satan tempted Jesus, he quoted the Bible. (Luke 4:1-13). What tools can you use to discern whether a plan is of God or Man or Satan?

Advent

1) When has an Advent, or any new beginning, renewed your faith?
2) What new disciplines or behaviors can you take on as Advent, or any other new beginning, approaches?
3) Consider: "No pain, no gain" at the gym and "No preparation, just blah" in our spiritual life.

Crisis in the Churches

1) If God were assessing some of the social issues of today, through what filters do you think He would be looking?
2) .How would applying God's filters to your own thinking change your views?
3) When have you known God to use unlikely individuals to do his work?
4) What stands in the way of your accepting individuals with differing beliefs or lifestyles?

Evangelism

1. In what ways do you already express caring for others?
2. Are you able to ask for the infilling of the Holy Spirit, and disciplined enough to wait for it?
3. What is the greatest gift of the Spirit (see the transition to I Corinthians 13 in I Cor 12:31)?

Chapter V – Churchy Stuff

Peter & Paul

1) How do you balance law and the "Spirit of Truth" in your own life?
2) When has your faith been strengthened by the differing views of others?
3) Paul said that the Law is the school-master to bring us to Christ. Are we forgetful upon "graduation?"

Beans & Rice

1) What religious traditions feed you spiritually?
2) What religious traditions interfere with your spiritual growth?
3) Do we all need the same balance of spiritual amino acids? Exactly the same balance?

Loaves & Fishes

1) What one thing could you do to encourage the future of the Church?
2) How does it feel to "expect a miracle?"
3) What happens if we are loving, welcoming, listening, sharing?
4) How often do you run into a church where question #3 is actually lived?

Tithing

1) Who were your role models for giving? Did they tithe?
2) Are you comfortable with your present plan of giving?
3) Is it right for the Churches to build beautiful buildings where the hungry shiver on the polished marble steps?

Big Ministries, Little Ministries

1) List some examples of 'little ministries' you are already doing. Are there others you would consider adding?
2) What inhibits you from outreach? What encourages you to participate?
3) Have you experienced any churches that emphasize ministries beyond the ordained? Anything different about them?
4) How do you answer: It's my church. I pay for it, and I expect to be ministered to properly!

Truth

1) Has anyone ever said to you that you have something in your life that s/he needs, and asked what it is and how to get it?
2) What would a plan to witness God's Truth look like?
3) Comment: Evangelism is one hungry beggar telling another where food can be found
4) What do you feel about the distinction between bringing a person to the church and bringing a person to Jesus?

Chapter V – Churchy Stuff

Interfaith Relations

1) Are you comfortable accepting people of different faiths? Why or why not? What are the obstacles?
2) List pairs of groups you consider polar opposites. What things do they have in common?
3) When do you find it difficult to love others? To love yourself? What thoughts or practices help to broaden your love?

The E Word

1) What is your personal definition of evangelism?
2) When has sharing your faith made a difference in the life of another?
3) Evangelism is usually built on a personal relationship of loving trust.
4) How good a listener are you for hearing personal needs being expressed?

The Governance of the Church

Part I: the Unanimity Rule

1) How are differences resolved in your Church's governing body?
2) How open are you to changing your mind when others seem to be sensing Truth that has not (yet) got through to you?
3) 3.Have you ever been in a group that waited silently for the Lord to speak to them, and clearly expected Him to do so?

Part II: the High Five

1) How would you rate the High-Five Rule: One, two, three, four or five?
2) Have there been times God has called you to be the naysayer in a group?
3) What do you feel when its getting late and your group agenda runs up against a naysayer?

Powers of Two

1) Do you believe that your life is better because of God's love? Do you believe the same can be true of others?
2) What inhibits you from reaching out to share your faith with others?
3) Mull: You have to listen and to feel to recognize those things in a friend's life that need God's loving touch.
4) How do you think God feels about your efforts?

Chapter VI - Addenda

This book, through years of production of a few copies at a time, grew steadily as new articles were added. Now the eBook version can continue that pattern, but printed copies are frozen in time.

New articles will be posted on the Website from time, and are accessible free of charge for the benefit of purchasers.

Author's Notes

All cited hymns (except one) are in the Hymnal 1982, according to the use of the Episcopal Church, Copyright © 1982, the Church Hymnal Corporation.

Most quotations from Scripture are from the Revised Standard Version, a few from the Authorized Version.

Many of these essays have been previously published in the Eastern Shore Episcopalian, a publication of the Diocese of Easton. Republished with permission.

Endnotes

[1] Praetium caritatis tu, Latin for the price of love is yourself. One of my father's favorite watchwords.

[2] Acts 17:6

[3] The behaviors of Father, Son and Holy Spirit as seen in Scripture are both male and female. For instance, Christ likens himself to a mother hen gathering her chicks. Historically, however, we refer to God by the male pronoun. I personally dislike the use of He/She, feel that It is entirely inappropriate, and that She is as restricted as He. So please forgive me if I offend by using the language I grew up with.

[4] 1 Corinthians 13:12

[5] Max Cleland, "Strong at the Broken Places," Chosen Books, 1980

[6] (Frankl June 1, 2006)".

[7] Alcoholics Anonymous, Third Edition, P. 449

[8] My father, the Rev'd William B. Stimson (1899-1972) wrote a memoir of these events under the same title. It was published (anonymously) in Holy Cross Magazine (Order of the Holy Cross, West Park, NY) in Volume LXXIII No. 8, August 1962, from which this article quotes extensively. Republished with permission

[9] This is a glimpse into my own spiritual journey. For me, it connects closely with Cleft Palate, the story of my father's healing.

[10] For those who don't know poker, a flush is a hand consisting of five cards, all of the same suit. It is a moderately valuable hand. Four of the same suite is valueless; a four-flusher is a person who bluffs – and occasionally wins.

[11] Thomas Hardy (1840-1928) Wessex Poems and other verses (1898)

[12] *The Seeing Eyes, Inc.,* Post Office Box 375, Morristown, New Jersey 07963-0375 USA

[13] William Blake (28 November 1757 – 12 August 1827) was an English painter, Poel and printmaker.

[14] C.S. Lewis. Attribution not found

[15] Hymn 490

[16] Peanuts, by Charles Schultz.

[17] The seven deadly sins are not a scriptural construct, but were developed over time by the Church Fathers. Therefore, they are not authoritative.

[18] Patrick Henry, speech before the Virginia House of Delegates, March 23, 1755.

[19] Admiral David G. Farragut at the Battle of Mobile Bay, August 5, 1864.

[20] Barry Goldwater, Republican candidate, during the presidential campaign of 1964.

[21] Erich Segal, "Love Story," (1970). The novel was adapted from the screen play in the same year. The most famous line from the film, "Love is never having to say you are sorry," was actually mis-spoken from the script. Originally the line was written: "Love is not ever having to say you are sorry," which does not sound substantially different to me.

[22] The first part of this tale has been circulating for decades: those in heaven feed each other and those in hell don't. The denizens of hell, many of them generally recognized as "good" people in their earthly life, surely knew they were capable of feeding each other. This reflections ponders their failings.

[23] Hymn 625, Stanza 3

[24] Abraham Lincoln, Second Inaugural Address, March 4, 1865

[25] From John Garvey's book, "Circles of Love", published in 1988, on Father Henri J.M. Nouwen's writings, P. 26 (Nouwen April 1, 2004)

[26] A meditation in Forward Day-by-Day used this railroad-track imagery.

[27] Harper & Brothers, 1948

[28] Hymnal 1940, #430

[29] Stephen F. Bayne, Bishop of Olympia, 1947-59

[30] Mathew 5:28

[31] Matthew 25:14-30; Luke 19:12-27

[32] Hymn 57

[33] Hymn 474, Stanza 4

[34] H. L. Mencken was for many years a journalist for the Baltimore Sun.

[35] Another parable I got from my father.

[36] The authenticity of this episode has been disputed.

[37] John S, Mogabgab devoted an issue of *Weavings* to the subject of vulnerability.

[38] D.Elton Trueblood 1900-94 American Quaker theologian and author.

[39] Martin Luther, Letter 99, paragraph 13, Erika Bullmann Flores

[40] C.S. Lewis, Letters, 23 April 1951

[41] Simone Weil, 1909-43, Simone Weil, French philosopher, Christian mystic, and social activist.

[42] Hymn 324

[43] Morton T. Kelsey (1917-2001) Episcopal priest, writer, lecturer

[44] Mere Christianity, bk 3, ch 10

[45] Hymn 541

[46] Hymn 671, Stanza 5

[47] Raymond A. Moody, Jr. (born June 30, 2944) is a psychologist and medical doctor.

[48] Elisabeth Kübler-Ross, MD (July 8, 1926 – August 24, 2004) was a Swiss-American psychiatrist
[49] Humphrey Carpenter, J.R.R. Tolkein: A Biography
[50] William Temple, 1884-1944, English bishop
[51] Lincoln Gettysburg Address, November 19, 1863
[52] In Biblical times, the Sanhedrin was the governing body of Israel, something like our Senate.
[53] The Caring Evangelism Program, a product of Stephen Ministries, St. Louis, MO.
[54] Hymn 652, Stanza 5
[55] An earlier version of this essay was published in The Living Church, January 9, 1994, under a different title. Republished with permission.
[56] A House of Commons speech on Nov. 11, 1947

Bibliography

Carpenter, Humphrey. *J.R.R. Tolkein: A Biography.* New York: Houghton Mifflin Company, June 2000.

Cleland, Max. *Strong at the Broken Places.* Boulder, CO: Taylor Trade Publishing, October 1, 2000.

Frankl, Viktor E. *Man's Search for Meaning.* Boston, MA: Beacon Press, June 1, 2006.

Lewis, C. S. *Letters of C. S. Lewis.* New York: Mariner Books, January 6, 2003.

Ministries, Stephen. *Caring Evangelism: How to Live and Share Christ's Love.* St. Louis: Stephen Ministries, 2010.

Nouwen, Henri J. M. *Circles of Love: Daily Readings with Henri J. M. Nouwen (Enfolded in Love).* London: Darton, Longman & Todd Ltd, April 1, 2004.

Segal, Erich. *Love Story.* New York: Avon, May 29, 2012.

Paul Stimson

About the Author

Paul Stimson's career was in engineering and oceanography. A collateral study of theology prompted occasional articles in his church's newsletter; feedback encouraged a monthly column which led in time to the writing of this book.

Paul's father, an Episcopal priest, died in 1972. About that time Paul drifted away from church; over the years many of Dad's words came back to him and formed the core of a new outlook. It has been wisely said that God has no grandchildren and we must all find our own path.

Most important, Dad had a profound sense of paradox--of what has been called the upside-down Kingdom, in which wealth is poverty, simplicity is wisdom, servanthood is freedom and weakness is power. Dad was an engaging preacher but he never wrote a book. In a sense this book is as much his as Paul's and the book is dedicated to him.

Mathews, Va.
June, 2014

Paul Stimson

www.ingramcontent.com/pod-product-compliance
Lightning Source LLC
LaVergne TN
LVHW051043080426
835508LV00019B/1682